A CANDL
Celtic

A Candle in the Darkness

Celtic Spirituality from Wales

PATRICK THOMAS

GOMER

First impression—1993
Second impression—1997

© text: Patrick Thomas
© illustrations: Janetta Turgel

ISBN 0 86383 974 6

The author's royalties from this book will be given to the St. Teilo Church (Brechfa) Centenary Appeal.

Printed by
Gomer Press, Llandysul, Dyfed, Wales.

Er cof am fy rhagflaenydd annwyl
ERIC MYRDDIN GREY
(Rheithor Brechfa a Ficer Abergorlech gyda
Llanfihangel Rhos-y-corn, 1960-83)

Cyfaill da ac offeiriad ffyddlon.

CONTENTS

Foreword   9

Introduction   11

Part One: Facing the Darkness
1: The Ruin of Britain   19
2: The Shadow of the Cross   32
3: The Splintered Spear   45

Part Two: The Language of Creation
4: Among the Birds and Animals   61
5: Standing Stones, Sacred Trees and Rain-making   74
6: The Healing Waters   87

Part Three: Learning to Love
7: Holy Mothers   103
8: Communities of Learning, Communities of Love   117
9: The Unexpected Glory   132

Conclusion   147

FOREWORD

In 1991 I wrote *The Opened Door*, a small booklet on Welsh Celtic spirituality. The book received a generous and enthusiastic welcome, both here in Wales and further afield. This prompted me to undertake a full-length study of the same subject. I am extremely grateful to Dr Dyfed Elis-Gruffydd and Gwasg Gomer for agreeing to publish it, and for the advice and help which they have given me.

Janetta Turgel's pictures for *The Opened Door* were highly praised and her illustrations for this volume are another example of her sensitive insight into the Welsh Celtic tradition. I have received much encouragement and support in my work on the book from Dr Rowan Williams (now Bishop of Monmouth), Dr George Noakes (formerly Archbishop of Wales), Canon A.M. Allchin, the Reverends Enid Morgan and Mandy Williams, Huw and Lynne Denman and Dominic and Rosie Carmichael.

I owe an immeasurable debt to those who have taught me to appreciate and love Welsh culture and the Welsh language, and particularly to my kindly and long-suffering parishioners in Brechfa, Abergorlech and Llanfihangel Rhos-y-corn, who are extraordinarily patient with their *'offeiriad llengar'*. For eight wonderful years I was able to turn to my cheerful and faithful predecessor in the three parishes, the Reverend Eric Grey, for friendship and wise counsel. Sadly he died while this book was being prepared for the press. It is dedicated to his memory.

As always my thanks and gratitude go to my wife Helen for her careful and perceptive comments on the book's development, and to our children, Iorwerth, Gareth, Llinos and Mair, who were very forbearing with a father who had become even more absent-minded than usual. Baby Gwenllian arrived while the book was still being written, bringing with her much joy and an even deeper appreciation of the importance of the *'pethau bychain'* in the economy of God's love.

Patrick Thomas
Rheithordy Brechfa
Gŵyl Sant Luc 1992

INTRODUCTION

I

hen George Carey was enthroned as Archbishop of Canterbury the person responsible for the television commentary on the ceremony remarked that the new Archbishop was 'the successor of St Augustine, who brought Christianity to Britain in 597 AD.' It was the kind of statement calculated to make Welsh, Irish and Scottish hackles rise, for there were Christians in Britain long before Augustine's mission. The spirituality of this earlier, Celtic expression of Christianity, particularly as it survived and developed in Wales, is the subject of this book.

After thirteen years of ministry in Welsh-speaking and bilingual churches and parishes I have come to believe that there is a discernable link between the earliest Welsh Christian spirituality and much of that which is most hopeful in modern Welsh religious life. By uncovering this continuity it may be possible to deepen our sense of identity as Welsh Christians, recovering the awareness that we are, in Waldo Williams' words 'keeping house in a cloud of witnesses' ('*Cadw tŷ mewn cwmwl tystion*'[1]), as the representatives in our own generation of a living spiritual tradition that spans the centuries.

Celtic spirituality has become a fashionable subject in recent years, particularly in England and the United States. This has led to some bizarre assertions by writers on the subject who have little or no direct connection with contemporary Celtic communities. The publisher's blurb on the cover of one recent anthology went so far as to claim that 'Composed in languages long extinct, Celtic literature has been inaccessible for many centuries.'[2] Such a remark shows a startling ignorance of (and possibly a hidden contempt for) the hundreds of thousands of people who continue to live and think and pray through the medium of the Celtic languages.

It is true that the distinctive cultures and languages of the Celtic lands have been increasingly marginalized and threatened during the modern period. But that in itself means that the Celtic Christian experience contains a special significance for a Western Christianity which is also increasingly under threat as it is pushed to the margins

11

of life. Despite centuries of often almost intolerable pressure exerted on it the Welsh linguistic and spiritual tradition has shown an astonishing resilience. As the folk singer Dafydd Iwan put it in a song commemorating sixteen hundred years of Welsh history:

Er gwaetha' pawb a phopeth,
Ry'n ni yma o hyd![3]
('In spite of everyone and everything, we are still here!')

II

elsh spirituality has its beginnings in the period of dislocation and chaos which followed the Roman departure from Britain. Historians and archaeologists continue to argue about what actually happened to those Britons living in what was to become eastern England. E.A. Thompson has recently persuasively challenged the view that the Saxon conquest of that area was a gradual and essentially peaceful process:

...if the Saxon invasion of eastern England were a matter of peaceful co-existence over a period of years, as is increasingly thought, how could we explain the disappearance of the place-names (other than those of prominent natural or manmade features —Roman cities, large rivers, hills, forests)? How could we account for the utter disappearance of the Celtic language from eastern England and of the Christian religion? How could we account for the fact that only about a score of nouns made their way from British Celtic into Anglo-Saxon and none at all from British Latin? Why did the Saxons fail to borrow as simple a device as the potter's wheel? Why did tens of thousands of Britons flee to the Continent as early as the 460s? Why was it that the Britons who survived in the west of the island conceived a hatred of the Saxons which the passage of generations and even of centuries did little to abate? Why, in fact, did they refuse to preach the Gospel to their tormentors even in the early eighth century, a fact which shocked Bede?[4]

As their culture and way of life caved in and disappeared before the invaders many Britons and Romano-Britons seem to have vanished

12

into a strange and terrifying 'black hole'. It suggests an experience as traumatic and appalling as the later disasters which inspired two of the masterpieces of early Welsh literature: the cryptic, heart-rending stanzas of the Heledd saga and the howl of pain that is Gruffudd ab yr Ynad Coch's lament for the last Llywelyn.

Such a trauma has a deep spiritual significance. Professor Walter Brueggemann, the American Old Testament scholar, has discerned three strands in the Book of Psalms. 'Psalms of orientation' reflect a serene, confident faith based on the certainty that 'some things are settled and beyond doubt, so that one does not live and believe in the midst of overwhelming anxiety.' Brueggemann remarks of such psalms that

> The problem with a hymnody that focuses on equilibrium, coherence and symmetry is that it may deceive and cover over. Life is not like that. Life is also savagely marked by disequilibrium, incoherence and assymetry.

The 'psalms of disorientation' reflect this painful and shattering experience: 'the move from an ordered, reliable life to an existence that somehow has run amok.' But Brueggemann also identifies a third group of psalms which 'bear witness to the surprising gift of new life just when none had been expected.' These he describes as 'psalms of new orientation.'[5]

For Brueggemann this movement from confident orientation through the agony of disorientation to the unexpected discovery of a new orientation reflects a basic pattern which is linked to spiritual growth and development both in the experience of individuals and of communities:

> The Psalms are not used in a vacuum, but in a history where we are dying and rising, and in a history where God is at work, ending our lives and making gracious new beginnings for us. The Psalms move with our experience. They may also take us beyond our own experience, into the more poignant pilgrimages of sisters and brothers.[6]

The British Celts underwent just such a pilgrimage during the fifth and sixth centuries. A terrifying disorientation replaced the former certainties as Romano-British society was swept away. And then, astonishingly, a new hope appeared. The process mirrored the emergence of a new orientation described by Brueggemann: 'the community of faith are . . . surprised by grace, when there emerges in present life a new possibility that is inexplicable, neither derived nor extrapolated, but wrought by the inscrutable power and goodness of God.'[7]

III

he theme of sudden disorientation, of the collapse of all certainty and security, has a place in the storytelling of many cultures. The Welsh equivalent of Adam and Eve's expulsion from Eden, or Pandora's disastrous opening of the forbidden box, occurs near the end of the story of Branwen in the *Mabinogion*. The seven survivors of the Welsh expedition to Ireland, accompanied by the talking head of their former chieftain Bendigeidfran, land on the island of Gwales (Grassholm). This inhospitable rock off the Pembrokeshire coast is now the home of an enormous colony of gannets. The storyteller, however, portrays it as an earthly paradise:

And at the end of the seventh year they set out for Gwales in Penfro. And there was for them there a fair royal place overlooking the sea, and a great hall it was. And they went into the hall, and two doors they saw open; the third door was closed, that towards Cornwall. 'See yonder,' said Manawydan, 'the door we must not open.' And that night they were there without stint, and were joyful. And notwithstanding all the sorrows they had seen before their eyes, and notwithstanding that they themselves had suffered, there came to them no remembrance either of that or of any sorrow in the world. And there they passed the fourscore years so that they were not aware of having spent a time more joyous and delightful than that. It was not more irksome than when they came there, nor could any tell by his fellow that it was so long a time. Nor was it more irksome having the head with them than it had been when Bendigeidfran was still alive. And because of those fourscore years it was called the Assembly of the Wondrous Head...

This is what Heilyn son of Gwyn did one day. 'Shame on my beard,' said he, 'if I do not open the door to know if that is true which is said concerning it.' He opened the door and looked on Cornwall and Aber Henfelen. And when he looked, they were as conscious of every loss they had ever sustained, and of every kinsman and friend they missed, and of every ill that had come upon them, as if it were even then that it had befallen them; and

14

above all else because of their lord. And from that moment they could not rest, save they set out with the head towards London . . . [8]

The great twentieth century Welsh poet David Gwenallt Jones based his poem '*Y Drws*' ('The Door') on this story. In it he compares the paradise which the seven men enjoyed on the island to the self-indulgent and fanciful literary aestheticism which was fashionable in his youth, when '*Yr heulwen ni threiddiai trwy ei rhamantaidd ffenestri/ Ar ecstasi'r gwleddoedd dandiaidd. . .*' ('The sunlight did not penetrate through [the hall's] romantic windows onto the ecstacy of the dandified feasts'). For Gwenallt, Heilyn is the one who opens the door to artistic, political and spiritual realism:

> *Ond Heilyn a agorodd y drws gwrthnysig:*
> *A chlywsom ddiasbad y wlad yn ei loes,*
> *Cyfarth coch y dwst diwydiannol;*
> *A gweled y bara, y gwin a'r Groes.* [9]

('But Heilyn opened the obstinate door: and we heard the cry of the country in its pain, the red barking of the industrial dust, and saw the bread, the wine and the Cross.')

In Gwenallt's poem Heilyn's action is seen as a blessing rather than a betrayal. It shatters the self-centred hedonism of a bogus paradise, forcing the seven to face up to the anguish of suffering humanity and the need to find an answer to its misery. Gwenallt points to 'the bread, the wine and the Cross' as the essential components of that answer: signs of hope for a people choking to death on industrial dust. Christ is not to be found in the unreality of Gwales, but his presence can be discerned in the pain of a disorientated and broken world. For Gwenallt, as for Brueggemann's Psalmist, true spiritual development involves finding a path through this often agonizing confusion to the new, profounder orientation that awaits on the far side. His interpretation of the Gwales story reflects the process that helped to form a distinct Christian spirituality in Celtic Wales.

In the chapters which follow I will attempt to identify the central strands of that spirituality, drawing on historical material, literary sources and the traditions which grew up around some of the key figures of the 'Age of the Saints' in Wales. [10] These traditions are not in themselves reliable historical data, though I will attempt to place them within an historical framework. The folklorist Elissa Henken described one of her recent books based on this material as 'a study not of the factual details of history but rather of the people's perception of history.'[11] In my view the stories told about the early Welsh saints also reflect a particular perception of Christianity and the spiritual life which has not yet entirely vanished from some corners of rural Welsh-speaking Wales. How that special way of seeing things evolved and came to be expressed is the theme of this book.

NOTES

[1] Waldo Williams, *Dail Pren* (Llandysul, 1956), p.67.
[2] Robert Van de Weyer, *Celtic Fire* (London, 1990).
[3] *Cadwn y Mur,* edited by Elwyn Edwards (Caernarfon, 1990), p.597.
[4] E.A. Thompson, *Saint Germanus of Auxerre and the End of Roman Britain* (Woodbridge, 1984), p.113.
[5] Walter Brueggemann, *The Message of the Psalms* (Minneapolis, 1984), pp.25, 51, 123-4.
[6] Walter Brueggemann, *Praying the Psalms* (Winona, 1986), p.24.
[7] Brueggemann, *Message of the Psalms,* p.124.
[8] *The Mabinogion,* edited by Gwyn Jones and Thomas Jones (London, 1949), pp.39-40.
[9] D. Gwenallt Jones, *Gwreiddiau* (Llandysul, 1959), p.18.
[10] Nora K. Chadwick, *The Age of the Saints in the Early Celtic Church* (London, 1963), p.5, defines the 'Age of the Saints' as 'the period from the late fifth to the late seventh century.'
[11] Elissa R. Henken, *Traditions of the Welsh Saints* (Cambridge, 1987), p.2.

PART ONE: FACING THE DARKNESS

Chapter One:

THE RUIN OF BRITAIN

1. 'Patrick, a sinner...'

ur only window into the thoughts and feelings of a fifth-century British Christian is a short confessional auto-biography. The author introduces himself with an anxious modesty that reflects the lack of self-assurance which is characteristic of both his surviving works: 'I am Patrick, a sinner, most uncultivated and least of all the faithful and most despised in the eyes of many.'[1] Patrick, son of a deacon and grandson of a presbyter, provides an important link between Romano-British Christianity and the churches which were to develop in the Celtic lands around the western seaways. He might well be described as the last of the Britons and the first of the Welsh. Sir Ifor Williams pointed out that 'There is considerable evidence that St Patrick swore in Welsh'—and he is thus the first recorded speaker of the language.[2]

Attempts to establish the dates of Patrick's life have led to a great deal of scholarly argument. One author attempted to solve the problem by suggesting that there were in fact two Patricks.[3] In a somewhat controversial study James Carney decided that Patrick was born in 418 and died in 493.[4] Bishop Patrick Hanson, however, basing his estimate on the internal evidence of Patrick's writings, feels able to conclude 'with some confidence' that he was born around the year 390 and died in about 460.[5] Patrick thus came into the world at a time when Roman Britain was in an acute state of crisis. The embattled Western Emperors were beginning to withdraw their forces to the Continent leaving Britain to the mercy of the invading Picts, Saxons and Irish. Four centuries of relative security and stability were at an end.

The breakdown of the old order was to have a shattering impact on Patrick's own life. When he was nearly sixteen years old his father's estate near the western coastal town of Bannavem Taberniae was raided by Irish pirates.[6] They captured Patrick and carried him off into slavery. From the account which he gives in his autobiographical *Confession* it is clear that only his faith sustained him in the loneliness of his captivity:

19

But when I had come by ill luck to Ireland—well every day I used to look after sheep and I used to pray often during the day, the love of God and fear of him increased more and more [in me] and my faith began to grow and my spirit to be stirred up, so that in one day [I would say] as many as a hundred prayers and nearly as many at night, even when I was staying out in the woods or on the mountain, and I used to rise before dawn for prayer, in snow and frost and rain, and I used to feel no ill effect and there was no slackness in me (as I now realize, it was because the Spirit was glowing in me). [7]

After several years of slavery Patrick escaped. The journey which followed was a difficult and dangerous one but eventually he was reunited with his parents. They begged him never to leave them again, but then Patrick had a very powerful dream in which a man named Victoricus gave him a letter entitled 'The Cry of the Irish'. He tells us that as he started to read it 'at that very moment I heard the voice of those who were by the Wood of Voclut which is near the Western Sea, and this is what they cried, as with one voice, "Holy boy, we are asking you to come and walk among us again," and I was struck deeply to the heart and I was not able to read any further and at that I woke up.' [8]

That vision ultimately led Patrick to return to Ireland. His *Confession* reveals that his mission there was marked by difficulties caused by enemies both inside and outside the church. He constantly refers to his own inadequacies and failures, though these are counter-balanced by an indomitable sense of God's love and care for him and an awareness of the Holy Spirit at work within him, making up for his own deficiencies. In a recent book Noel Dermot O'Donoghue has presented Patrick as a mystic in the classic Christian mould, a forerunner of St John of the Cross. [9] This may be something of an overstatement. Patrick's tortuous pilgrimage, fraught as it was with periods of darkness, anxiety and fear, is too untidy (and thus, in a sense, too representative) to be neatly fitted into the textbook categories of mystical development. That may be what gives his Confession its lasting value. '*Patricius, peccator rusticissimus*', weak, fallible and totally dependent on God's love to keep him going, is a figure with whom many ordinary Christians can readily identify.

A revealing parallel can be drawn with a later writer whose reflections on his own spiritual pilgrimage struck a chord in the hearts of thousands of eighteenth century Welsh Christians. The Carmarthenshire poet William Williams, Pantycelyn, wrote in one of his hymns:

Disgwyl wyf trwy hyd yr hirnos
Disgwyl am y bore ddydd,
Disgwyl clywed pyrth yn agor
A chadwynau'n mynd yn rhydd:
Disgwyl golau
Pur yn nh'wyllwch tewa'r nos.

Daw, fe ddaw y wawr wen olau
Nes bo'r cwmwl du yn ffoi,
Tarth a niwl yn cyd-ddiflannu
Ag oedd wedi cyd-grynhoi:
Dyma'r oriau
Wy'n eu gweled draw drwy ffydd. [10]

('I am waiting through the long night, waiting for the morning, waiting to hear the gates opening and the chains being loosed, waiting for pure light in the deepest darkness of night. It will come, the white light of dawn will come and force the black cloud to flee away, the mist and fog that had gathered together will disappear together: these are the hours that I see ahead through faith.')

Patrick's favourite description of Christ is as 'the true sun', the power of resurrection. Like William Williams he sees the light of Christ as a force that can liberate him from the power of sin, despair and death. [11] The fifth-century bishop and the eighteenth-century hymnwriter are linked by their awareness of their total dependence on Christ to rescue them from the darkness of a treacherous and uncertain world.

That treachery and uncertainty is underlined by the only other document whose authorship can be reliably ascribed to Patrick: *The Letter to Coroticus*. Coroticus (Ceredig) was a Romano-British chieftain. Hanson suggests that he was probably *tyrannus* (king) of Strathclyde in what is now Scotland. [12] He was a Christian, but this did not stop him from brutally attacking a group of Patrick's newly baptized Irish converts, killing many of them and selling the survivors to the pagan Picts as slaves. The letter, excommunicating 'Coroticus and his gang of criminals, rebels against Christ', is Patrick's response to this horrific event. His sense of helplessness and despair stems from his realization that the faith which should have built a bridge between the Irish and their neighbours has not done so. He laments to his converts:

O most beautiful and beloved brothers and children whom I have begotten in Christ [whose numbers] I cannot count, what am I to

21

do for you? I am not capable of assisting God or men. The wickedness of the wicked has prevailed over us. We have been treated like outsiders. Perhaps they do not believe that we have the same God as Father. They think it derogatory that we are Irish. As the text says, Do you not have one God? Why has each one deserted his neighbour?[13]

His disillusionment with his own people leads Patrick to identify himself with the Irish even though he had described himself earlier in the letter as 'a slave in Christ to an outlandish nation.'[14]

Patrick's writings testify to the chaos of the period in which he lived. What remained of Romano-British civilization was threatened both by outside enemies and by internal divisions. Nominally Christian warlords like Coroticus would ignore or scorn the demands of the Gospel whenever it suited their self-interest to do so. Patrick's own experience of his fellow Christian leaders both in Ireland and Britain seems to have been marked by squabbles, petty rivalries and acts of betrayal. Yet in the midst of the confusion and darkness a light of hope still burns—the faith that inspired and upheld one fifth-century Briton:

> . . . you have worked in me with such divine power so that today I should regularly exalt and glorify your name wherever I happen to be not only when things go well but also in troubles, so that whatever may happen to me whether good or bad I am equally bound to give thanks to God because he has shown that I should believe in him endlessly as trustworthy . . .[15]

2. 'A victory by faith . . .'

ne historian has described south-eastern Britain in the year 429 as 'a still rich but defenceless society.'[16] Shortly afterwards that society was destroyed so effectively that almost all memory of it was erased. Writing about the sixth-century historian Gildas' view of the recent past, E.A. Thompson comments:

> The great collapse had taken place less than a century previously; yet no one could now explain what it was which had happened or how it had happened. Of the four hundred years of the Roman occupation of Britain men knew now of little more than that kings

across the sea had once ruled the island. Their governors had been harsh. There had been a great persecution of Christians and a ruler called Magnus Maximus. And that was practically all. . . . Knowledge of the outside world and knowledge of the past had been wiped out of men's minds.[17]

One of the few historical facts that survives from the twilight of the fragile Romano-British community is that it was visited by Germanus, Bishop of Auxerre, in 429. He later paid another visit, probably in the 440s.[18]

Germanus was apparently invited to Britain by a group within the British Church who wanted to refute the claims made by the followers of Pelagius. Pelagius (Morgan to the Welsh) has been described as 'the first-known major British writer and theologian.'[19] He began teaching in Rome in the 380s. When the city was threatened by Alaric and the Goths he fled to Carthage and eventually ended up in Palestine where he died around 430. Some of his views were condemned as heretical by the Council of Carthage in 411 and in the following year St Augustine of Hippo began to write against him. It is clear that by the 420s Pelagius had a considerable following in his homeland, possibly including some of the local bishops. Germanus' task was to bring the British Church back into the orthodox fold.

The rough-and-ready popular version of Pelagianism tended to stress salvation by one's own efforts rather than through dependence on God's love, though this represents a distortion of Pelagius' own views.[20] Germanus underlined his arguments for the human need of God's grace by actions which demonstrated the power of that grace. The most spectacular of these was the bloodless defeat of an invading army of Picts and Saxons. Bede's account of the battle, which took place just after Easter, stresses the part played by the faith of the British soldiers. They had put themselves under the authority of Germanus and his fellow bishop Lupus and 'under these apostolic leaders, Christ himself commanded in the camp.' Most of the soldiers were newly baptized: 'Strong in faith and fresh from the waters of Baptism, the army advanced; and whereas they had formerly despaired of human strength, all now trusted in the power of God.'[21]

Germanus and his men ambushed the invading army. As the Picts and Saxons advanced into the trap which had been set for them, the bishops shouted 'Alleluia!' three times. The British army then joined in the shout, terrifying the invaders, who seem to have thought that the end of the world had suddenly come. They ran for their lives, leaving their weapons behind them. After previous defeats and humiliations the Britons had won an astonishing victory: 'The scattered spoils were collected, and the Christian forces rejoiced in the triumph of heaven. So the bishops overcame the enemy without bloodshed, winning a victory by faith and not by force.'[22]

The 'Alleluia Victory' turned out to be more than a lesson in applied theology. Its immediate importance was slight. E.A. Thompson notes: 'This was a small-scale action, and R.H. Hodgkin was probably right to call it a 'skirmish'.'[23] But in Wales, as Germanus increasingly became identified with Garmon, the founder of several churches in Powysland, the victory took on a new significance. In the seventeenth century Bishop Ussher relocated the 'Alleluia' battlefield at Maes Garmon, near Mold (Yr Wyddgrug) in Flintshire. This identification was accepted by several generations of Welsh historians including Theophilus Evans in the eighteenth century and Thomas Price ('Carnhuanawc') in the nineteenth.[24] Germanus' triumph became seen as a crucial victory for the Welsh (as the descendants of the Britons) at a time when they faced extinction and for Christianity at a time when it was threatened by heresy from within and paganism from without.

The Welsh reworking of the Germanus/Garmon story achieved its finest expression in *Buchedd Garmon* ('The Life of Garmon'), a radio play based loosely on Constantius' original Life of St Germanus. The play was written by Saunders Lewis, one of the greatest Welsh dramatists, poets and critics of the twentieth century, during the period when he was about to stand trial at the Old Bailey for setting fire to an R.A.F. bombing school in the Llŷn peninsula. A Welsh jury had been unable to reach a verdict when Lewis and his two co-defendants were tried in Caernarfon, and the case had therefore been transferred to London. The burning of the bombing school was a protest against the threat to Welsh culture in its heartland. Lewis drew a parallel between the crisis facing Wales in 1936 and that facing Garmon/Germanus and the Britons in 429:

> *Garmon, Garmon,*
> *Gwinllan a roddwyd i'm gofal yw Cymru fy ngwlad,*
> *I'w thraddodi i'm plant*
> *Ac i blant fy mhlant*
> *Yn dreftadaeth dragwyddol;*
> *Ac wele'r moch yn rhuthro arni i'w maeddu.*
> *Minnau yn awr, galwaf ar fy nghyfeillion,*

Cyffredin ac ysgolhaig,
Deuwch ataf i'r adwy,
Sefwch gyda mi yn y bwlch,
Fel y cadwer i'r oesoedd a ddêl y glendid a fu.
A hon, fy arglwydd, yw gwinllan d'anwylyd di
Llannerch y ffydd o Lan Fair i Lan Fair.
A ddoi dithau i arwain fy myddin i Bowys draw? [25]

('Garmon, Garmon, Wales my country is a vineyard given to my care, to be handed on to my children and to my children's children as an eternal inheritance; and see the pigs rushing in to defile it. I now call on my friends, commoners and scholars, come with me to the gap, stand with me in the breach, so that the beauty that was may be kept for the ages to come. And this, my lord, is the vineyard of your beloved, the clearing filled with faith from Llan Fair [Mary's Church] to Llan Fair. Will you come to lead my army over to Powys?')

For Lewis' Garmon the battle has a two-fold significance: to defend the nation and to preserve the faith.

Canys arnom ni
Disgynnodd dydd yr amddiffyn,
Dydd y ddeublyg amddiffyn,
Dydd adeiladu'r Gristnogaeth a chadw'r ffin. [26]

('For on us fell the day of defence, the day of the two-fold defence, the day of building Christianity and keeping the border.')

He succeeds in his struggle and the dramatist links Garmon's Eastertide victory with Christ's resurrection:

Dydd atgyfodiad Crist,
Dydd rhyddid eneidiau'r mad
A'u harwain o Limbo drist,
Yw dydd gwaredigaeth ein gwlad.

Llawen fo Cymru'n awr;
Daeth ar ei thywyllwch wawr,
Ac o garchar ofn daeth yn rhydd. [27]

('The day of Christ's resurrection, the day of freedom for the souls of the good and their leading forth from sad Limbo, is the day of our country's salvation. May Wales be happy now; dawn came on her darkness and she came forth free from the prison of fear.')

The victory won by the historical Germanus was no such liberating turning-point. The Romano-British community to whom he had preached was soon not even a memory. Gildas records a desperate letter sent by the Britons to the Roman consul Aëtius in 446, only seventeen years after the bishop's triumph: 'To Aëtius, thrice consul: the groans of the British... The barbarians push us back to the sea, the sea pushes us back to the barbarians; between these two kinds of death, we are either drowned or slaughtered.' 'But they got no help in return,' he comments laconically.[28] Germanus was not succeeded by any other helpful or friendly visitors from the Continent and by the time that Constantius wrote his biography of the saint communications between Gaul and the south-east of Britain had long been severed.[29]

The story of the 'Alleluia Victory' nevertheless survived as a small ray of hope from a dark and terrifying time. Against all the odds a battle had been won 'by faith and not by force' by an army that 'trusted in the power of God'. In the midst of the misery and destruction that overwhelmed the Romano-British community in the south-east such a sign may easily have been lost sight of. The fact that Garmon/Germanus has resurfaced as a significant figure in the embattled Welsh culture of the twentieth century suggests that his emphasis on trusting in God even in apparently hopeless situations can still be a source of strength and inspiration.

3. 'This tearful history...'

Gildas, according to his Breton biographer, was a native of Arecluta, 'a part of Britain [which] took its name from a certain river called the Clut, by which that district is, for the most part, watered.'[30] This suggests that he came from the Clydeside region, the area once ruled by Patrick's opponent Coroticus. With the extinction of Romano-British society in south-east Britain, the Scottish Lowlands and Cumbria (still known to the Welsh as 'Yr Hen Ogledd'—'The Old North') became the cradle of a newly emerging Welsh culture. As this region came under increasing pressure many of its people migrated to what is now Wales. Their arrival may not always have been welcome. Rhiannon's rather dim suitor in Pwyll Pendefig Dyfed, the South Welsh first branch of the Mabinogi, is 'Guawl uab Clut, gwr tormynnawc, kyuoethawc' ('Wall son of Clyde, a wealthy man with a host of soldiers at his call').[31] The evident satisfaction which the author takes at the humiliation of this arrogant intruder by Rhiannon and Pwyll indicates a certain prejudice against '*Gŵyr y Gogledd*'—'the Men of the North'.

In his main surviving work, *The Ruin of Britain,* written around the year 540, Gildas notes that he was born forty three years earlier, in the year in which Ambrosius Aurelianus (Emrys Wledig) defeated the Saxons at Badon Hill.[32] This victory had led to a period of relative stability. The country was now divided between the Britons and the Saxons. The latter seem to have had complete control over south-eastern Britain. Gildas lamented that because of 'the unhappy partition with the barbarians' the shrine of Alban, the British proto-martyr, was now in pagan territory.[33] The historian was painfully aware of the sufferings of his people in the years before Ambrosius' rebellion:

All the major towns were laid low by the repeated battering of enemy rams; laid low, too, all the inhabitants—church leaders, priests and people alike, as the swords glinted all around and the flames crackled. It was a sad sight. In the middle of the squares the foundation-stones of high walls and towers that had been torn from their lofty base, holy altars, fragments of corpses, covered (as it were) with a purple crust of congealed blood, looked as though they had been mixed-up in some dreadful wine-press. There was no burial to be had except in the ruins of houses or the bellies of beasts and birds.....a number of the wretched survivors were caught in the mountains and butchered wholesale. Others, their spirit broken by hunger, went to surrender to the enemy; they were fated to be slaves for ever, if indeed they were not killed straight away, the highest boon. Others made for lands beyond the sea; beneath the swelling sails they loudly wailed, singing a psalm that took the place of a shanty: 'You have given us like sheep for eating and scattered us among the heathen'. Others held out, though not without fear, in their own land, trusting their lives with constant foreboding to the high hills, steep, menacing and fortified, to the densest forests, and to the cliffs of the sea coast.[34]

The half century of respite won by Badon Hill had not repaired the damage inflicted by the invaders: 'the cities of our land are not populated even now as they once were; right to the present they are deserted, in ruins and unkempt. External wars may have stopped, but not civil ones.'[35]

Gildas' 'tearful history' was not primarily a record of past tragedies. They were included as a dreadful warning to his contemporary

27

audience. His main concern was with 'the evils of the age.'[36] He could see his people heading for another disaster as appalling as that which had effectively wiped out the south-eastern Britons. With considerable savagery he attacks those whom he feels are responsible for this impending catastrophe. Perhaps it is not surprising that in Brittany, his final resting place, Gildas has come to be regarded as the saint to be invoked by sufferers from rabies, or that at Mellionnec his feast used to be marked by a specially arranged dog fight.[37]

The source of Gildas' anger was his sense of the moral and spiritual corruption that was characteristic both of the secular and the ecclesiastical leaders of the Britons: 'Britain has kings, but they are tyrants; she has judges, but they are wicked . . . Britain has priests, but they are fools; very many ministers, but they are shameless; clerics, but they are treacherous grabbers.'[38] 'The final victory of our country that has been granted to our times by the will of God' was in jeopardy because of the way in which these men indulged themselves at the expense of their people, becoming 'slaves of the belly, slaves, too, not of Christ. . . but of the devil.'[39]

In his denunciation of these people Gildas reveals himself as a spokesman for the ideals of the monastic movement which became increasingly influential among the Britons during his lifetime. A 'preface on penance' attributed to Gildas survives which reveals the discipline which the author expected his fellow monks to abide by.[40] The asceticism involved was strict but not extreme. As Dr Wendy Davies comments on one of its provisions, 'it is not unduly hard; and if eggs, cheese, fat and vegetables formed the stuff of penitential diet the normal diet for professed monks must have been palatable and quite substantial.'[41] According to his Breton biographer Gildas' personal regime was much more austere: 'we have learnt from a trustworthy source, that he took a most scanty food for his body . . . he buffetted his body with frequent fastings and protracted vigils. . .'[42] The picture presented by his other biographer, Caradog of Llancarfan, is even harsher (though not unlike that recorded in the other medieval Welsh saints' lives), portraying Gildas as a hermit in the mould of St Antony of Egypt. Caradog claims that Gildas prayed clad in goat's skin, lived on fresh-water herbs and barley-bread mixed with ashes, never took a bath and went into a river at midnight to say the Lord's Prayer three times. His Victorian editor remarks that 'this representation of Gildas as an eremite. . . seems a purely legendary addition.'[43]

Nevertheless there is no doubt that Gildas played an important part in the development of the ascetic movement in Ireland and Brittany as well as in Wales. His prediction of the imminent threat to the corrupt and quarrelsome British kingdoms proved only too accurate. In the twenty years after the appearance of *The Ruin of Britain* the Saxons began a relentless push forward into the British heartland.[44] As the next phase of the British collapse developed the monastic movement became one of the few remaining sources of hope for the Britons of Wales, Devon and Cornwall. One of the proverbs ascribed to Gildas (who was becoming known as 'Gildas the Wise' in the Celtic lands) was *'Navi fracta, qui potest natare natet'*—'When the ship is holed, let the man who can swim swim.'[45] By 540 the British ship was indeed far from seaworthy. Gildas knew that, unless a radical change of heart took place, the 'Ruin of Britain' would soon be complete, and only a few hardy swimmers sustained by faith in God would survive.

The century and a half between Patrick's birth and Gildas' stark warning to the leaders of the surviving Romano-British kingdoms was a period of traumatic change. In 390 Romano-British society was still intact and apparently stable—although the danger signs were already on the horizon. Fifty years later Germanus would visit the vulnerable, defenceless remnants of that society in south-east Britain, momentarily filling them with hope. But within a hundred years that fragile community had vanished. The shrine of St Alban, at which Germanus had paid his respects, was in pagan Saxon territory, lost to the Britons forever—and Gildas the British historian was unaware that Germanus had ever visited these shores. Gildas was however agonizingly aware of the horrors which had stained the half-century before he was born. His pain and anger were increased by the fear that they represented only the first chapter in a continuing history of destruction.

Even so, there was still an element of hope, however dark the encroaching night might sometimes seem. By the middle of the sixth century the monastic movement of which Gildas was a part had become firmly established in the Celtic lands. It had its beginnings in a reaction against the worldliness of the church, which had led Antony and his followers to flee into the solitude of the Egyptian desert in the third and fourth centuries. Because of its roots and ideals and the forms which it took it was far better able to cope with the pressures and dangers of a collapsing society than was the urban and villa based church which developed in Roman Britain. It was among those involved in this movement of monks and hermits that a distinctive

Welsh spirituality began to develop, and it was to those associated with it that Gildas addressed the prayer at the end of *The Ruin of Britain*:

May the almighty God of all consolation and pity preserve the very few good shepherds from all harm, and, conquering the common enemy make them citizens of the heavenly city of Jerusalem, that is, of the congregation of all the saints. . .[46]

Had he been aware of them, he would doubtless also have included in his prayer that small but courageous remnant of British Christians who continued to cling to their religion in the areas occupied by the pagan Angles, Saxons and Jutes. Evidence of their survival against all the odds has been uncovered in recent years by archaeologists, one of whom describes it as 'witness to the faithfulness of the few in a time of great adversity.'[47]

NOTES

[1] R.P.C. Hanson, *Life and Writings of the Historical Saint Patrick* (New York, 1983), p.76.

[2] Sir Ifor Williams, *The Beginnings of Welsh Poetry*, edited by Rachel Bromwich (Cardiff, 1980), p.14.

[3] Thomas F. O'Rahilly, *The Two Patricks* (Dublin, 1971).

[4] James Carney, *The Problem of St Patrick* (Dublin, 1973).

[5] Hanson, *Life and Writings*, p.25.

[6] Hanson, *Life and Writings*, p.19, remarks that 'we shall probably never know exactly where Patrick's home was. All we can say is that it must have been near the western or the southwestern coast of Britain to be exposed to raids from Irish pirates and if we are to be guided by the statistics of villas so far discovered it is more likely to have lain in the south than the north of the country.'

[7] Hanson, *Life and Writings*, p.86.

[8] Hanson, *Life and Writings*, p.92.

[9] Noel Dermot O'Donoghue, *Aristocracy of Soul: Patrick of Ireland* (London, 1987).

[10] *Emynau Williams Pantycelyn*, selected by Derec Llwyd Morgan (Gregynog, 1991), p.58.

[11] Hanson, *Life and Writings*, pp.90, 122.

[12] Hanson, *Life and Writings*, p.11.

[13] Hanson, *Life and Writings*, p.70.

[14] Hanson, *Life and Writings*, p.66.

[15] Hanson, *Life and Writings*, p.104.

[16] J.N.L. Myres, *The English Settlements* (Oxford, 1986), p.210.

[17] Thompson, *Germanus of Auxerre*, pp.114-5.

[18] Thompson, *Germanus of Auxerre*, pp.55-70, makes a case for the second visit having taken place in 447.

[19] M. Forthomme Nicholson, 'Celtic Theology: Pelagius' in *An Introduction to Celtic Christianity*, edited by James P. Mackey (Edinburgh, 1989), p.388.

[20] James P. Mackey, 'Is there a Celtic Christianity?' in *An Introduction to Celtic Christianity*, pp.17-18.

[21] Bede, *A History of the English Church and People,* translated by Leo Sherley-Price (Harmondsworth, 1965), p.62.

[22] Bede, *History,* p.63.

[23] Thompson, *Germanus of Auxerre,* p.46.

[24] Theophilus Evans, *Drych y Prif Oesoedd,* Part One, edited by Samuel J. Evans (Bangor, 1902), p.87; Thomas Price ('Carnhuanawc'), *Hanes Cymru a Chenedl y Cymry* (Crickhowell, 1842), p.198.

[25] Saunders Lewis, *Buchedd Garmon* (Llandysul, 1957), p.48.

[26] Lewis, *Buchedd Garmon,* p.42.

[27] Lewis, *Buchedd Garmon,* pp.52-3.

[28] Gildas, *The Ruin of Britain and other works,* edited and translated by Michael Winterbottom (London, 1978), pp.23-4.

[29] Thompson, *Germanus of Auxerre,* p.86.

[30] *Two Lives of Gildas,* translated by Hugh Williams (Felinfach, 1990), pp.13-15.

[31] *Pedeir Keinc Y Mabinogi,* edited by Sir Ifor Williams (Cardiff, 1964), p.14.

[32] Gildas, *The Ruin of Britain,* p.28.

[33] Gildas, *The Ruin of Britain,* p.19.

[34] Gildas, *The Ruin of Britain,* pp.27-8.

[35] Gildas, *The Ruin of Britain,* p.28.

[36] Gildas, *The Ruin of Britain,* p.36.

[37] Per Jakez Hélias, *Dictionnaire des Saints bretons* (Paris, 1985), p.155.

[38] Gildas, *The Ruin of Britain,* pp.29, 52.

[39] Gildas, *The Ruin of Britain,* pp.16, 28-9.

[40] Included in Gildas, *The Ruin of Britain,* pp.84-5.

[41] Wendy Davies, *Wales in the Early Middle Ages* (Leicester, 1982), p.151.

[42] *Two Lives of Gildas,* p.25.

[43] *Two Lives of Gildas,* pp.86-7.

[44] Myres, *The English Settlements,* pp.162-3.

[45] Gildas, *The Ruin of Britain,* pp.82, 145.

[46] Gildas, *The Ruin of Britain,* p.79.

[47] Dorothy Watts, *Christians and Pagans in Roman Britain* (London, 1991), p.226.

Chapter Two:

THE SHADOW OF THE CROSS

1. 'There is no desert place.'

he tiny chapel of St Govan is wedged in a cleft halfway down a cliffside on the Pembrokeshire coast, not far from the village of Bosherston. It was built during the Middle Ages on the site of a cell once occupied by a sixth-century Irish hermit. Govan (Gofan in Welsh and Gobán in Irish) may well have been a disciple of Ailbe (Aelfyw) the bishop from Munster who is said to have baptized St David.[1] He was one of those who had been influenced by that same ascetic movement which Gildas saw as providing hope for the reformation and renewal of the decadent British Church.

The first Christian hermit may have been St Paul the Hermit (otherwise known as Paul of Thebes), who died c.341. The figure, however, who was to become the father of Christian asceticism was St Antony of Egypt (251?-356), whose retreat into the desert inspired a great many disciples. Explaining the background to this development Derwas Chitty wrote:

> . . .*anachoresis* was in the air in the third century in Egypt—men, sometimes whole communities, withdrawing into the deserts or swamps to escape from the intolerable burden of taxation and the public liturgies. The Christians just had another reason for the same course of action. It might be that some of the stranger ascetic practices like the wearing of chains could reflect a time when the fugitives were going into training for martyrdom.
>
> But the Peace of the Church brought an extra incentive to the ideal of monastic renunciation. Pagan and Christian alike had been inspired by the example of the martyrs. In the new worldly security of the Church, the Christian would seek to recover the old martyr spirit; while the pagan, brought to the Faith by what he had seen of the life and death of Christians in time of persecution, would seek a way of not less absolute devotion to Christ.[2]

It seems probable that the influence of this movement reached Ireland, Wales and south-west Britain directly from the Eastern

Mediterranean. Charles Thomas has shown that pottery was brought by sea from Alexandria and Carthage to these areas in the period between 450 and 530.[3] The earliest dateable monastery in the British Isles was established at Tintagel in Cornwall between 470 and 500, which suggests a possible link with the trade route. As Thomas remarks, 'Where. . . platters and amphorae could travel, so too could pilgrims to and from the Holy Land, occasional refugees, books and ideas.'[4]

There is some evidence of a cult of St Antony of Egypt in South Wales. Ffynnon Sant Antwn (St Antony's Well) survives at Llanstephan on the shore of Cardigan Bay. There is a possibility that the well may be connected with a local sixth-century hermit who had named himself after the saint whose life he wished to emulate.[5] St Antony and St Paul the Hermit feature on a panel of a ninth-century cross-slab at Nash in Glamorgan.[6] They are also mentioned in an anonymous poem of praise to the Trinity which was included in the thirteenth century *Llyfr Du Caerfyrddin* ('Black Book of Carmarthen'):

> *Duu y enu in vn.*
> *Duu paul ac annhun.*[7]

('God whose name is one; God of Paul and Antwn.')

The spirit of the hermit movement is summed up in a verse from another poem in Llyfr Du Caerfyrddin:

> *ym brin in tyno. in inysset mor*
> *im pop fort it elher*
> *rac crist guin nid oes inialet.*[8]

('On the hill, in the valley, in the islands of the sea, everywhere you may go, before blessed Christ there is no desert place.')

In their search for 'white martyrdom' (as opposed to the 'red martyrdom' undergone by those killed during the times of persecution) the ascetics fled from a corrupting world and a corrupted church to the most lonely and desolate places that they could find. They settled in forests, on clifftops and 'in the islands of the sea.' And yet, as the poet noted, they then discovered that with Christ there was 'no desert place.' Their solitude was transformed by their awareness of his presence.

The most spectacular of the island monastic settlements was on Skellig Michael, a rock jutting out of the Atlantic eight and a half miles off the coast of Kerry. It was probably founded by St Suibhne of Skellig, perhaps as early as the sixth century. Despite being raided by the Vikings several times the community on Skellig Michael continued for several centuries.[9] A modern Irish fisherman who has spent his life fishing the waters around the Skellig rocks has commented on the difficulties that must have faced the courageous souls who settled on one of them:

How these ascetic monks contrived to live on this island is a mystery by today's standards. In summer, no doubt, they enjoyed seabirds, eggs and fish but winter must have brought months of lean isolation. The small hide-covered boats of the period were hardly adequate for a regular supply ferry; perhaps there was more arable soil on this 44 acre crag in olden times than there is today.[10]

Govan in his cleft in the Pembrokeshire cliffside can hardly have fared much better.

The stories told about the Pembrokeshire hermit portray him as someone who, out of love for God and his neighbour, had become an amateur but highly effective coastguard.[11] The rocks around what is now St. Govan's Head are extremely dangerous. Govan seems to have taken it upon himself both to warn passing ships of the potential hazard and to help any shipwrecked survivors who came to land in the vicinity of his cell. There was a fresh water spring just below his cell, so that he could give the unfortunates something to drink. No doubt, like the Skellig monks, he also had a seasonal supply of birds, eggs and fish which he could use to feed them.

Govan's humanitarian activities seem to have aroused the hostility of some of his neighbours. Impoverished coastal communities on inhospitable coastlines have often depended on a mixture of piracy, 'wrecking', and the despoiling (and even the murder) of the ship-wrecked as a way of supplementing their meagre income. This appears to have been true of some of the inhabitants of the south Pembrokeshire coast in Govan's time. Seeing the hermit as a threat to their livelihood, a group of these pirates decided to kill him. When his would-be murderers arrived however, Govan hid in a crevice in the rock, praying to God to help him. The rock, so it is said, then closed around him, keeping him safe until his enemies grew tired of searching and went away.

Govan's hiding-place can still be seen behind the medieval chapel, with a step leading up to it through an opening to the left of the altar. The shape of the crevice roughly resembles that of a human being, with marks in the rock which became regarded as the impression of

Govan's ribs. Over the centuries local folk superstition began to attribute special qualities to it: it is still said that anyone who makes a wish whilst turning in the space will find that the wish is granted before the year is out.

There is, however, a much more profound significance to this sanctuary in the cliff-face. It is a symbol of Govan's personal helplessness and his total dependence on God for defence and succour in a dangerous and chaotic world. This vulnerability was an essential element of the 'white martyrdom' of the Celtic hermits. In part it was an imitation of God's deliberate self-limitation in Christ: the supreme risk taken in love which led to the agony of Calvary. It also reflected the type of faith expressed in some of the psalms:

> For God alone my soul waits in silence,
> for my hope is from him.
> He alone is my rock and my salvation,
> my fortress; I shall not be shaken.
> On God rests my deliverance and my honour;
> my mighty rock, my refuge is God.
> Trust in him at all times, O people;
> pour out your heart before him;
> God is a refuge for us. [12]

At a time of social dislocation and disorder the idea that God represented a sure and dependable refuge had a very strong appeal, particularly when it could be related to the experience of individual Christians. Govan's story offered hope to many threatened people unable to help or defend themselves.

2.   'The despised Cynog. . .'

Foolishness for Christ's sake has its roots in Scripture. Paul told the Corinthians that 'the word of the cross is folly to those who are perishing, but to us who are being saved it is the power of God. . . For the foolishness of God is wiser than men and the weakness of God is stronger than men.' He also reminded them that 'God chose what is foolish in the world to shame the wise, God chose what is weak in the world to shame the strong, God chose what is low and despised in the world, even things that are not, to bring to nothing things that are, so that no human being might boast in the presence of God.' [13]

This idea of 'the foolishness of God' became linked to the figure of Christ being ridiculed by the soldiers before his crucifixion:

And the soldiers led him away inside the palace (that is, the praetorium); and they called together the whole battalion. And they clothed him in a purple cloak, and plaiting a crown of thorns they put it on him. And they began to salute him, "Hail, King of the Jews!" And they struck his head with a reed, and spat upon him, and they knelt down in homage to him. And when they had mocked him, they stripped him of the purple cloak, and put his own clothes on him. And then they led him out to crucify him. [14]

Jesus, mocked and spat upon, became identified in Christian minds with the 'suffering Servant' mentioned by Isaiah:

...he had no form or comeliness that we should look at him,
and no beauty that we should desire him.
He was despised and rejected by men;
a man of sorrows, and acquainted with grief;
and as one from whom men hide their faces
he was despised, and we esteemed him not. [15]

The powerful image presented by these passages has always had its appeal for the more radical elements of Western Christianity (a notable example being some of the English Quakers and Ranters of the mid-seventeenth century). Its greatest impact, however, has been on Eastern Christianity, particularly in Russia. The services in celebration and commemoration of different types of holy men and women in the Russian Orthodox Church include 'The General Service to the Foolish for Christ's Sake', while Nadejda Gorodetzky has shown the importance of the humiliated Christ in nineteenth century Russian literature and thought. [16] A recent study by John Saward has also sought to discover examples of folly for Christ in the early Irish tradition. [17]

Saward makes much of the figure of Suibne Geilt, an Irish king who is said to have gone mad during the battle of Magh Rath in 637. His madness was supposed to be the result of a curse put on him by St Rónán, after Suibne had flung the holy man's psalter in a lake. In his distraction Suibne took to living in the tree tops until he was eventually befriended by St Moling, who gave the dying king communion on his death-bed and blessed him. [18] Nora Chadwick has suggested a link between the Irish tree-dwelling king and a small group of Eastern ascetics known as 'Dendrites' or 'tree-dwellers', one

36

of the most noted of whom was 'a monk Adolas who came from Mesopotamia and dwelt in a large plane tree and made a window through which he used to talk to visitors.'[19]

There are problems with this theory, not least because the story of Suibne itself is apparently derived, at least in part, from the tradition of Myrddin Wyllt, who became mad after the battle of Arfderydd in Cumbria (573) and thereafter lived a wild existence in the forest of Celyddon.[20] The confusion is compounded by the survival of a description of a meeting between St Kentigern (Cyndeyrn) and a naked hairy madman in a wood. The madman, whose name was Lailoken (Llallawg), had lost his senses during a terrible battle at a place called Carwannok.[21] Suibne, Myrddin and Lailoken are all recorded to have seen a vision in the sky during their respective battles. Lailoken seeks to be reconciled to the Church by Kentigern (as Suibne was by Moling) just before his death. Several scholars now suggest that the Lailoken story is the oldest of the three, with its origins in the British kingdom of Ystrad Clud (Strathclyde) and that the other two tales derive from it.[22] It thus seems a very insecure basis on which to build any theory about Irish tree-dwelling 'fools for Christ'.

A rather more promising Irish figure, also discussed by Saward, is the 'lamb-witted' Mac-dá-Cherda, who was cursed by a druid and as a result 'his hair fell out and he lost his mind and reason and sense, so that he became a mad foolish senseless fool, who preferred any other fool to the people of the world.'[23] Mac-dá-Cherda's folly is interspersed with moments of deep insight and wisdom. There is no doubt that he sees his condition as God given and therefore is conscious of himself as being in some sense a 'fool for Christ':

> If there is truth in the happy end
> which Jesus has ordained for the fool,
> if foolishness is what God loved,
> is wisdom any better than foolishness?[24]

Even Mac-dá-Cherda's madness is something imposed from outside, rather than the deliberate adoption of foolishness in imitation of Christ. One figure who does indeed seem to represent this kind of self-imposed folly is a Welsh holy man who has escaped Saward's notice. Cynog was the eldest son of Brychan, the mid-fifth century king of Brycheiniog, whose family became one of the three saintly tribes of Wales.[25] Hugh Thomas (1673-1720), the Breconshire herald and antiquary, recorded the legend of Cynog from 'the poor Ignorant Country People' in or around the year 1702.[26] He writes of Cynog:

> In his youthfull days forsaking this World for the next, he retired from his Fathers Court to a Cott or Hermitage not far from the high Roade betweene Brecknock and Battle, about a mile from Carevong his fathers Metropolitan City...where he traviled up and downe in a poor miserable Habit and made himself a heavy boult or Ring of Iron for his head roughly twisted togather like a Torce or Wreath insteed of a Crowne of Gold.... This rendered him...the Scorne and Derition of all that saw him from which he was nick named Kynog Camarch that is the Dispised Kynog.[27]

In the rest of the story, as recorded by Thomas, Cynog uses his torque to defeat some 'Ormests' or giants who are oppressing the local people, a blacksmith who tries to smash the torque on his anvil is killed when a splinter from it pierces his brain, and the saint himself is finally murdered by some of his fellow hermits.[28]

Elissa Henken notes two other versions of the origin of Cynog's torque. According to a fifteenth-century *cywydd* by Hywel ap Dafydd ap Ieuan ap Rhys it was a '*torch o nef*' ('a torque from heaven'), while *De Situ Brecheiniauc* says that Brychan took it from his own arm to give his son after the boy's baptism.[29] Giraldus Cambrensis (Gerallt Gymro) describes a torque which he had seen which was said to be Cynog's:

> From its weight, texture and colour one would think that it was gold. It is made of four sections, as you can see from the joins, wrought together artificially by a series of weldings and divided in the middle by a dog's head, which stands erect with its teeth bared.... On the torque there is the mark of a mighty blow, as if someone had hit it with an iron hammer. A certain man, or so they say, tried to break the collar for the sake of the gold. He was punished by God, for he immediately lost the sight of both eyes.[30]

This relic has not survived, though Sir T.D. Kendrick suggested, on the basis of Giraldus' description, that it was probably Welsh or Irish work from the tenth or eleventh century, considerably after Cynog's time.[31] It was also clearly very different to the 'heavy Boult or Ring of Iron...roughly twisted togather' which Cynog wore 'insteed of a Crowne of Gold' in the folk tradition recorded by Hugh Thomas.

The Cynog of folk memory was very much a 'fool for Christ's sake,' with his crude iron torque echoing the Crown of Thorns. Like

38

Isaiah's suffering Servant he was 'despised and rejected by men,' and had apparently deliberately chosen to make himself the object of their scorn and derision. For the eldest son of a king to behave in this way suggests a very conscious protest against the way power had come to be seen in his society. Gildas portrays the British kings of the mid-sixth century as violent, venial and corrupt. It may be that, by choosing the path of a very different Lord, Cynog was attempting to make a prophetic point to his contemporaries. Foolishness for Christ's sake is in fact a deeper wisdom that is only visible to those who can see the shallowness of much that the world accounts wise. The extant legend of Cynog is the story of a king's son who sets aside his golden crown and its privileges to share the vulnerability and pain of his people. The same story is at the heart of the Christian Gospel.

3. 'An ecstasy of self-denial.'

ne of the more startling developments within fourth-century Christianity had been the growth of the cult of the martyrs, centred around particular shrines. Peter Brown remarks that

...the Christian Mediterranean and its extensions to the east and northwest came to be dotted with clearly indicated *loci* where Heaven and Earth met. The shrine containing a grave or, more frequently, a fragmentary relic, was very often called quite simply, 'the place'. . . . It was a place where the normal laws of the grave were held to be suspended. In a relic, the chilling anonymity of human remains could be thought to be still heavy with the fullness of a beloved person. [32]

This growing interest in martyrs and their relics had an impact on the Romano-British Church. Bede notes that at Verulamium, the scene of the death of the British protomartyr Alban during Diocletian's persecution, 'When the peace of Christian times was restored, a beautiful church worthy of his name was built.' [33] He also records that Germanus, during his first visit to Britain, deposited 'relics of all the Apostles and several martyrs' in Alban's tomb, and 'took away with him a portion of earth from the place where the blessed martyr's blood had been shed.' [34]

In the sixth century Gildas was still very much aware of the significance of Alban's shrine for British Christians. Writing of Diocletian's persecution he says:

God....acted to save Britain being plunged deep in the thick darkness of black night; for he lit for us the brilliant lamps of holy martyrs. Their graves and the places where they suffered would now have the greatest effect in instilling the blaze of divine charity in the minds of beholders, were it not that our citizens, thanks to our sins, have been deprived of many of them by the unhappy partition with the barbarians. I refer to St Alban of Verulam, Aaron and Julius, citizens of Caerleon, and the others of both sexes who, in different places, displayed the highest spirit in the battle-line for Christ. [35]

The tide of invasion which had swept over eastern Britain had been so overwhelming that few memories from Roman times survived for Gildas to write down. It is therefore particularly significant that he was still able to record the story of Alban's death in some detail. Alban had rescued a fugitive priest, giving him shelter and changing clothes with him in order to draw off the man's pursuers. Gildas describes this action as being 'in imitation...of Christ, who laid down his life for his sheep...'[36]

'Red martyrdom' was thus as important a concept to sixth-century Welsh Christians as was the 'white martyrdom' associated with the ascetic movement. One of those who is mentioned as having suffered the fate of a 'red martyr' is Gildas' brother, Caffo, a monk who had settled in Anglesey. Caffo was a disciple of Cybi, but the two of them fell out, probably as a result of Gildas' ferocious denunciation of Maelgwn Gwynedd, the ruler who had become Cybi's patron. Deprived of Cybi's protection, Caffo was murdered by some shepherds from Rhosfyr (Newborough), who were apparently servants of Maelgwn's wife. The place where he died was known for a long time afterwards as 'Merthyr Caffo'.[37]

Other martyrs of the period include the victims of pagan pirates and (less creditably) those who were killed by their fellow monks out of rivalry or jealousy. One unfortunate, around whom a cult developed in Pembrokeshire and elsewhere, was a boy named Tyfai, said to have been Teilo's nephew, who was killed while attempting to protect a swineherd from an outraged farmer whose crops had been damaged by the serf's pigs.[38] The single most significant group of martyrs, however, consist of women, whose position was often extremely vulnerable, particularly when they felt called to the hermit life.

The most famous of these women martyrs was Gwenfrewi (Winefred) around whom a major cult developed in the Middle Ages. According to legend her head was cut off by her rejected suitor Caradog, but put back on again shortly afterwards by her uncle Beuno. Beuno apparently had a gift for restoring the heads of those who had been decapitated: he performed the same kindness for Tegiwg and her husband.[39] Baring Gould and Fisher do their best to de-mythologize Gwenfrewi's story:

> What really happened was probably no more than this, that Winefred ran away from Caradog, he overtook her, and in the struggle she was wounded by him in the throat, but was easily cured by her mother and Beuno.[40]

Given this reading of the story it seems safest to set Gwenfrewi on one side for the moment (she will reappear in a later chapter) and focus on another sixth century woman martyr, Eluned or Eiliwedd.

Our knowledge of Eluned depends almost entirely on a manuscript account by the seventeenth century Breconshire herald Hugh Thomas, the man who also recorded local traditions about Cynog. Thomas portrays her as a young woman who from her earliest childhood had decided to devote herself to God's service. When a princely suitor appeared who was favoured by her parents, Eluned ran away in disguise and tried to find refuge in the nearby villages. She was rejected at Llanddew, treated as a common thief at Llanfillo and scorned at Llechfaen, where no one would give her lodging and she had to lie down in the road. As a result she decided to become a hermit and was permitted to build a cell on a wooded hill near Brecon. Unfortunately her spurned lover tracked her down and killed her. She was buried in her cell, which was converted into a chapel.[41]

By 1188, when Giraldus Cambrensis accompanied Archbishop Baldwin on a journey through Wales to recruit men for the Third Crusade, the cult of Eluned was long established. Speaking of churches dedicated to the daughters of Brychan Brycheiniog (of whom Eluned was one), he says:

> One is on the top of a hill in Brecknockshire, not far from the main castle of Brecon. It is called the church of Saint Eluned, after the name of the saintly virgin who on that spot refused the hand of an earthly ruler and married instead the King Eternal, thus triumphing in an ecstasy of self-denial.[42]

An element of this ecstasy seems to have been passed on to some of those who gathered at the church on the first of August each year to celebrate Eluned's feast-day. Giraldus describes them dancing

41

between the graves, collapsing on the ground, jumping in the air and miming with their hands and feet whatever work they had broken the sabbath commandment with (ploughing, cobbling, tanning, spinning and weaving). Eventually they would all go into the church, be absolved and return to normal. The scene depicted by Giraldus is not unlike some of the eighteenth century accounts of the 'jumpers' in Daniel Rowland's church at Llangeitho at the height of the Methodist Revival.

That the example of the martyrs remained in the Welsh consciousness is shown by a manuscript account of the life and sufferings of the Roman Catholic martyr Richard Gwyn (or White), who was brutally executed in Wrexham in 1584. The author of the account (probably John Bennett) writes:

And is it any wonder, the people knew his innocency being well acquainted with the good man's conversation ye space of XXtie years together, they knew his cause to be just and honest being directly for religion. They knew ye example to be rare, the like never heard of in Wales since the death of S. Winefride, traceing therein the happy steppes of his blessed country man Saint Albano, the first martyr of the ancient Britons and proto martyr of this Iland. [43]

The author underlines the link between Richard Gwyn/White and 'his blessed country man' by noting in the margin that 'Albanus is white in English.'

More recently the signifance of martyrdom has been expressed in a remarkable poem by Waldo Williams, the Pembrokeshire Quaker. 'Wedi'r Canrifoedd Mudan' ('After the Dumb Centuries') is written in praise of Richard Gwyn and two other Welsh Roman Catholic martyrs, John Roberts of Trawsfynydd and John Owen the carpenter. The poet regards them as windows into eternal life:

Maent yn un â'r goleuni. Maent uwch fy mhen
Lle'r ymgasgl, trwy'r ehangder, hedd. Pan noso'r wybren
Mae pob un yn rhwyll i'm llygad yn y llen. [44]

('They are one with the light. They are above my head where peace gathers through the vastness. When night darkens the sky each one provides an eyehole through which I can glimpse beyond the veil.')

Through their suffering and death the martyrs become one with the suffering Christ:

Y diberfeddu wedi'r glwyd artaith, a chyn
Yr ochenaid lle rhodded ysgol i'w henaid esgyn
I helaeth drannoeth Golgotha eu Harglwydd gwyn.[45]

('The disembowelling after the torture of the hurdle, and before the sigh where a ladder was given for their soul to ascend to the broad expanse of the tomorrow of their blessed Lord's Golgotha.')

For Waldo, as for Richard Gwyn in the sixteenth century and Gildas in the sixth century, martyrdom breaks down the barrier between the world of time and the world of eternity, revealing God's light in the midst of the deepest darkness.

NOTES

[1] Henken, *Traditions of the Welsh Saints,* pp.38, 259.
[2] Derwas Chitty, *The Desert a City* (New York, 1966), p.7.
[3] Charles Thomas, *Celtic Britain* (London, 1966), pp.57-60.
[4] Charles Thomas, *Britain and Ireland in Early Christian Times AD 400-800* (London, 1971), p.88.
[5] 'Llanstephan a'i Hynafiaethau: Ffynnonau Cyssegredig—Ffynnon Sant Antwn', *Yr Haul,* XI (1867), p.114.
[6] Siân Victory, *The Celtic Church in Wales* (London, 1977), p.63.
[7] *Llyfr Du Caerfyrddin,* edited by A.O.H. Jarman (Cardiff, 1982), p.17.
[8] *Llyfr Du Caerfyrddin,* p.15.
[9] Des Lavelle, *Skellig—Island Outpost of Europe* (Dublin, 1981), pp.12-14.
[10] Lavelle, *Skellig,* p.14.
[11] For the stories about Govan see Henken, *Traditions of the Welsh Saints,* pp.258-9 and Patrick Thomas, *The Opened Door: A Celtic Spirituality* (Brechfa, 1990), [p.25]; also S. Baring Gould and J. Fisher, *The Lives of the British Saints,* 4 vols (London, 1907-13), III, 143-7.
[12] Psalm 62. 5-8 (RSV).
[13] 1 Corinthians 1. 18, 25, 27-9 (RSV).
[14] Mark 15. 16-20 (RSV).
[15] Isaiah 53. 2b-3 (RSV).
[16] *The General Menaion,* translated by N. Orloff (London, 1899), pp.272-82; Nadejda Gorodetzky, *The Humiliated Christ in Modern Russian Thought* (London, 1938).
[17] John Saward, *Perfect Fools: Folly for Christ's Sake in Catholic and Orthodox Spirituality* (Oxford, 1980), pp.31-47
[18] An attractive recent translation of the Suibne saga is Seamus Heaney, *Sweeney Astray* (London, 1984).
[19] Chadwick, *Age of the Saints,* p.110.
[20] *Trioedd Ynys Prydein: The Welsh Triads,* edited by Rachel Bromwich (Cardiff, 1961), pp.469-70.
[21] Nikolai Tolstoy, *The Quest for Merlin* (London, 1985), p.27.
[22] *Ymddiddan Myrddin a Thaliesin,* edited by A.O.H. Jarman (Cardiff, 1967), p.46.
[23] 'Life of St Cuimine Fota', quoted by Saward, *Perfect Fools,* p.39.
[24] 'Life of St Cuimine Fota', quoted by Saward, *Perfect Fools,* p.40.

43

[25] *The Dictionary of Welsh Biography* (London, 1959), p.56.
[26] Baring Gould and Fisher, *Lives*, II, 266.
[27] Baring Gould and Fisher, *Lives*, II, 266.
[28] Baring Gould and Fisher, *Lives*, II, 266-8.
[29] Henken, *Traditions of the Welsh Saints*, pp.180-1.
[30] Gerald of Wales, *The Journey Through Wales and The Description of Wales*, translated by Lewis Thorpe (Harmondsworth, 1980), p.86.
[31] *Dictionary of Welsh Biography*, p.92.
[32] Peter Brown, *The Cult of the Saints* (London, 1981), pp.10-11.
[33] Bede, *History*, p.47.
[34] Bede, *History*, pp.60-1.
[35] Gildas, *The Ruin of Britain*, p.19.
[36] Gildas, *The Ruin of Britain*, p.19.
[37] Baring Gould and Fisher, *Lives*, II, 50.
[38] Baring Gould and Fisher, *Lives*, IV, 289.
[39] Baring Gould and Fisher, *Lives*, IV, 218.
[40] Baring Gould and Fisher, *Lives*, III, 191.
[41] Hugh Thomas' account is reproduced in Baring Gould and Fisher, *Lives*, II, 419-20.
[42] Gerald of Wales, *The Journey*, p.92.
[43] *The Welsh Elizabethan Catholic Martyrs*, edited by D. Aneurin Thomas (Cardiff, 1971), pp.125-6.
[44] Waldo Williams, *Dail Pren*, p.90.
[45] Waldo Williams, *Dail Pren*, p.91.28.

Chapter Three:

THE SPLINTERED SPEAR

1. 'A saint because of his spear...'

The death through treachery of Prince Llywelyn the Last ('*Ein Llyw Olaf*') at Cilmeri in 1282 was one of the darkest moments in Welsh history. It elicited a powerful and emotional lament from the poet Gruffudd ab yr Ynad Coch, who saw the event in apocalyptic terms:

> *Poni welwch chwi hynt y gwynt a'r glaw?*
> *Poni welwch chwi'r deri yn ymdaraw?*
> *Poni welwch chwi'r môr yn merwinaw*   *'r tir?*
> *Poni welwch chwi'r gwir yn ymgweiriaw?*
> *Poni welwch chwi'r haul yn hwyliaw*   *'r awyr?*
> *Poni welwch chwi'r sŷr wedi r' syrthiaw?*
> *Poni chredwch chwi i Dduw, ddyniaddon ynfyd?*
> *Poni welwch chwi'r byd wedi r' bydiaw?*[1]

('Do you not see the course of the wind and rain? Do you not see the oak trees clashing together? Do you not see the sea clawing at the land? Do you not see the truth arming itself? Do you not see the sun sailing through the sky? Do you not see that the stars have fallen? Do you not believe in God, foolish men? Do you not see that the world is endangered?')

In looking back through history for a similar tragedy the poet referred to '*Llawer llef druan fal ban fu Gamlan*' ('Many a wretched cry as happened at Camlan'). Brynley Roberts notes that Arthur's disaster at Camlan had become 'the symbol of irreversible, calamitous defeat.'[2]

Camlan is not mentioned in the ninth century *Historia Brittonum* of Nennius, the earliest source of material about Arthur, but it does appear in an entry in the tenth-century *Annales Cambriae* under the year 537: 'The Battle of Camlann in which Arthur and Medraut fell: and there was plague in Britain and Ireland.'[3] Any reference to King Arthur is fraught with historical difficulties. As Thomas Charles-Edwards puts it in a recent assessment of the evidence, 'there may well have been an historical Arthur. . . the historian can as yet say nothing valuable about him.'[4] Nevertheless early Welsh story-telling included a significant body of material about Arthur's last battle, dating from long before the fanciful twelfth-century imaginings of Geoffrey of Monmouth:

Even in the native tradition it would appear that the circumstances of Arthur's death, real or apparent, were the tragic consequences of plotting, dissension at court, and perhaps a nephew's betrayal. There may well have been a *chwedl* (saga) of Camlan. . . . which was. . . an integral part of the Welsh legend of Arthur.[5]

Perhaps the battle is best seen in the context of the civil wars among the Britons which Gildas refers to as taking place during the period of peace with the Saxons after the victory of Badon Hill.[6] It was the apparently trivial incident which had caused the conflict, and its tragic and disastrous outcome, which led to Camlan being included among the '*Tri Ouergat Ynys Prydein*' ('Three Futile Battles of the Island of Britain') in the Welsh Triads. The other two 'Futile Battles' were Cad Goddeu ('The Battle of the Forest'), a mythical fight between Amaethon fab Dôn and Arawn king of Annwfn (the parallel world in Welsh Celtic mythology), and the historical battle between two rival British factions at Arfderydd (Arthuret in Cumbria) in 573, during which Myrddin was said to have been driven mad by the horror of the slaughter.[7]

There are two different Welsh traditions about the number of men who survived the battle of Camlan. Either there were only three survivors (including Cynwyl, the saint connected with Cynwyl Gaio and Cynwyl Elfed in Carmarthenshire) or there were seven. The longer list includes four others who came to be regarded as saints: Cynfelyn, Cedwyn, Derfel and Pedrog.[8] Of these Pedrog or Petroc is in many ways the most interesting. In the description of the twenty-four knights of Arthur's court in Peniarth MS 127 he is named as one of the '*Tri Chyvion Varchoc*' ('Three Just Knights'):

Three Just Knights were in Arthur's Court: Blaes son of the Earl of Llychlyn, and Cadog son of Gwynlliw the Bearded, and Pedrog Splintered-Spear, son of Clement Prince of Cornwall. The peculiarities of those were that whoever might do wrong to the weak, they contended against him who did him wrong in the cause of justice; and whoever might do wrong they slew, however strong he might be. For those three had dedicated themselves to preserve

46

justice by every Law; Blaes by earthly Law, Cadog by the Law of the Church, and Pedrog by the Law of arms. And those were called Just Knights.[9]

Pedrog is normally identified with the Cornish hermit Petroc, who, according to Baring Gould and Fisher, 'has left a deeper impress on the West of England than any other Saint.'[10] A life of the Cornish Petroc was written by John of Tynemouth, who includes an extraordinary description of his subject's travels in which Petroc journeys across the sea in a silver bowl, lives for seven years on a single fish which is caught, cooked, eaten and then miraculously returned to its original condition each day, finally returning to Cornwall with a tame wolf at his side and founding a monastery at Bodmin.[11] There is no mention of his ever having been a soldier.

The Pedrog of Welsh tradition is a very different character. He is regarded as the son of a Cornish king whereas, curiously enough, the Petroc connected with Cornwall and the West of England is said to be of Welsh origin.[12] The Welsh epithet consistently used to describe Pedrog is '*Paladrddellt*' ('Shattered-Spear'), and, as Elissa Henken has pointed out, he and Derfel are the soldier-saints most frequently referred to by fifteenth-century Welsh poets.[13] '*Gwawe pedrok*' ('Pedrog's spear') was still preserved as a relic in Llanbedrog parish church in 1535.[14] Lewys Glyn Cothi (fl. 1447-89) may have had this object in mind when he said of one of his patrons:

> Pedrog Llan Dyvrïog vryn
> Yw 'r milwr â 'i wayw melyn.[15]

('The soldier with his yellow spear is the Pedrog of Llandyfriog hill.')

The fullest account of the story of Pedrog and his spear appears in a *cywydd* written by Dafydd Nanmor (fl. 1460) invoking the saint's aid to get rid of a vast quantity of sand which a storm had blown across the land at Tywyn, near Pedrog's church of Y Ferwig.

> Yng Nghamlan o 'r Bryttaniaid,
> Yr oydd eb ladd o 'r ddwy blaid
> Seithwyr o 'r maes a aethant.
> Vn sydd wrth ei waew yn sant.
> Pedroc, oedd enwoc â 'i ddûr,
> Vawrweirthioc, wrth varw Arthvr.
> Mab brenin, o vrenhinoydd
> Kernyw gynt, coronawc oydd.

47

Gwasnaethv bv, ac y bydd,
Y Drindawd, wedy'r vndydd,
Vwch Dofr, a rroi diovryd
Arver byth o arfau'r byd.
Yna i troes i'r mann y tric
Duw j varw hyd y Verwic. [16]

('In Camlan there were seven of the Britons who went from the field without being killed. One is a saint because of his spear: Pedroc who was famous with his precious steel weapon at Arthur's death. He was a crowned king's son—of the ancient kings of Cornwall. After that day he served (and will serve) the Trinity above Dover (?) and renounced the use of worldly weapons forever. Then he came to Y Ferwig, the place where he lived to his dying day.')

The reference to Dover is strange. Perhaps '*Dofr*' should really read '*dwfr*' ('water'). Pedrog may have become a cliff-dwelling hermit 'above the water' before eventually settling at Y Ferwig in Cardiganshire.

Rachel Bromwich believes that Dafydd Nanmor's account of the saint's career is based on local Cardiganshire traditions. [17] Whether or not this is so, it depicts Pedrog as a renowned warrior who suddenly and dramatically turns his back on the weapons of war, presumably because of a disgust with 'Futile Battles' and their needless slaughter. Taliesin's description of the battle of Argoed Llwyfain conveys the grimness of sixth century warfare:

A rac gweith argoet llwyfein
bu llawer kelein.
Rudei vrein rac ryfel gwyr. [18]

('And in front of Argoed Llwyfain there were many corpses. The crows were turned red because of the warriors')

Pedrog's broken spear was a symbol of his disgust at such a sight. It signified a rejection of the values and beliefs which were taken for granted by the earliest Welsh poets whose work survives: Taliesin and Aneirin, writing around the year 600. The evidence of other figures connected with sixth century Wales suggests that Pedrog's story reflects a wider movement that questioned the compatibility of Christianity and warfare.

2. 'Will this be your custom and your history?'

aliesin and Aneirin were the poets of what Nora Chadwick has called 'The British Heroic Age.' She writes of their work:

> The poems are concerned with the deeds of heroes, individual men whose prowess in battle and loyalty to their leaders, or generosity to their followers, has made them worthy of the praise of the bard. [19]

The greatest of these poems is '*Y Gododdin*', Aneirin's record of the disastrous raid on Catraeth (Catterick) by three hundred British warriors who had ridden south from Edinburgh. There seem to have been only four British survivors, one of whom was Aneirin himself. [20] The British warband were Christians:

> *Gwyr a aeth gatraeth oedd fraeth eu llu.*
> *glasved eu hancwyn a gwenwyn vu.*
> *trychant trwy beiryant en cattau.*
> *a gwedy elwch taweluch vu.*
> *ket elwynt e lanneu e benydu.*
> *dadyl dieu agheu y eu treidu.* [21]

('The men who went to Catraeth were a swift host. They feasted on fresh mead, it was their poison. Three hundred men fighting under orders, and after rejoicing there was silence. An inescapable meeting with death overtook them, even though they went to churches to do penance.')

Their Christianity may have been of the somewhat superficial and defective kind associated with their compatriot Coroticus/Ceredig, the Strathclyde chieftain whose brutality had so appalled Patrick.

However it is not long before an element of criticism of the unthinking 'heroic' acceptance of slaughter and annihilation begins to appear in early Welsh poetry. This may partly be the result of war-weariness, but it is also linked to the growing importance of the ascetic movement in the Celtic lands. Some hints of this new approach occur in a cycle of poems from Powys which it is now generally agreed once formed part of a saga about Llywarch Hen. The poems refer to the death of Llywarch's twenty-four sons, all of whom had been urged by their aged father to go into battle against the invading English.

Llywarch himself is an irritating but ultimately tragic figure. He sends his sons to their deaths in the service of an heroic ideal which he

49

may well not have lived up to during his own career as a fighting man. Jenny Rowlands remarks of Llywarch:

His reputation as an undaunted champion, it must be remembered, depends solely on his own testimony; throughout he is shown as long past his prime. Although undoubtedly he was at one time a warrior, it appears that in looking back he vastly inflates his past deeds, inflating in turn present expectations for his sons. He urges them to do no less than what he claims to have done himself. But the odds are against Llywarch having performed what he claims to have done since he has survived to old age while all twenty-four of his sons are killed in youth. 'Marwnad Gwên' shows that the death of his last surviving son awakened him to the reality of his exaggerated expectations. It is likely that the poet intended Gwên's forceful counterattack in the dialogue, his clear view of the assumptions which were driving him to his death, as a catalyst in Llywarch's awakened self-knowledge equal to the shock of loss. [22]

Llywarch's lament for the last of his sons reveals the final bankruptcy and barrenness of the heroic ideal:

Pedwarmeib ar hugeint a ueithyeint vygknawt
Drwy vyn tauawt lledesseint.
Da dyuot vygcot colledeint. [23]

('Because of my tongue the twenty-four sons whom my flesh nurtured were killed. The coming of a little [fame] is good. They have been lost.')

As Sir Ifor Williams remarks, Llywarch 'ends the Death Song of all his hopes with one word, standing apart, one word complete with the finality of utter despair, *Colledeint.* They have all been lost. They have perished, every one of them.' [24]

Tucked away among a group of gnomic verses in the thirteenth-century *Llyfr Du Caerfyrddin* is an *englyn* which refers to one of Llywarch's sons. Apparently his father is accusing him of cowardice:

Nid vid iscolheic, nid vid e leic unben,
nyth eluir in dit reid;
och, Gindilic, na buost gureic. [25]

('You are not a scholar, you are not a lord white-haired with age, you are not called upon in the day of need—a pity, Cynddilig, that you were not a woman!')

50

Clerics, women and the aged (who included, of course, Llywarch himself) were free from the obligation to fight. Llywarch's sneering insult inspired Thomas Gwynn Jones (1871-1949) to write 'Cynddilig', one of the most powerful anti-war poems ever composed in Welsh.

In the poem Cynddilig has become a monk at Meifod in Powys. He is shown searching the battlefield of Rhyd Forlas to find the body of Gwên, the last of his brothers. His father's sarcastic taunt still echoes in his memory, and is renewed when Cynddilig and the old chieftain meet. But then when the two of them reach Meifod, Cynddilig intervenes to protect a terrified slave-girl who runs into the monastic enclosure in a desperate attempt to escape from a band of Mercian soldiers:

> *A chyfododd y mynach ei law a gofyn yn dawel:*
> *"Ai camp gennych yw ymlid y caeth*
> *a gorfod ar y sawl ni ddwg arfau?*
> *ai hyn fydd eich defod a'ch hanes?"*
>
> *Hwythau, tewi a wnaethant*
> *yn eu syndod, canys undyn*
> *ni safai rhag nifer a'u herio,*
> *heb arf yn y byd,*
> *heb nac ofn na bod iddo neb yn gyfnerth...*
> *ai dewr ai ynfyd oedd?*
>
> *A'r mynach wedi arhoi am ennyd*
> *wyneb yn wyneb â hwy,*
> *a droes at y gaethes ac a drwsiodd*
> *y brath oedd drwy fôn ei braich.* [26]

('And the monk raised his hand and quietly asked, "Do you think it a great feat to chase after slaves and force yourselves on the unarmed? Will this be your custom and your history?" They, astonished, became silent, for one man would not stand against several and challenge them, without a weapon in the world, without fear, without anyone to support him...was he brave or a fool? And the monk, having stayed face-to-face with them for a second, turned to the slave girl and dressed the wound in her upper arm.')

The Mercians withdraw feeling ashamed, but one of them fires a parting shot which kills Cynddilig. Llywarch finally recognizes his son's courage and grieves for him—while far above fly three *colomen*

51

wen wâr ('gentle/civilized white doves'): Llywarch's son Gwên and his Mercian enemy who had killed one another during the battle, and the peace-loving Cynddilig. Three souls finally united and at peace with one another.

It is significant that Thomas Gwynn Jones should have portrayed Cynddilig as one of the monks of Meifod. The most prominent figure connected with Meifod was Tysilio, son of Brochwel Ysgithrog, prince of Powys. The Breton sources used by Baring Gould and Fisher state that Tysilio became a monk at Meifod against the wishes of his father, who had intended him to be a warrior. Later, after his brother's death, Tysilio had to flee to Brittany to avoid his widowed sister-in-law who wanted to marry him and make him prince.[27] This view of the saint is somewhat at odds with that presented in '*Canu Tyssilyaw*', a poem by Cynddelw Brydydd Mawr (fl. 1155-1200). Cynddelw portrays Tysilio as a fierce fighter who took part in the battle of Cogwy, which has been identified with Maserfeld, fought between Penda of Mercia and Oswald of Northumbria in 642. Both Ifor Williams and Henry Lewis have pointed out that it is historically impossible that Tysilio was at Maserfeld.[28] Elissa Henken has observed of Cynddelw's poem: 'The saint is viewed in heroic terms and has heroic virtues, but some of the imagery can be dismissed simply as heroic language resorted to by the poet.'[29]

One possibility that may reconcile the two very different portraits of the saint is that Tysilio, like Pedrog, was a soldier who at some point rejected the heroic tradition and turned to the monastic life, refusing to have anything more to do with warfare. This would link him with the critical approach to heroic ideals reflected in the Llywarch Hen poems, which were apparently written in Powys, Tysilio's home. It would seem that Tysilio of Meifod and Thomas Gwynn Jones' imaginary monk from the same *clas* had more than a little in common. This idea is reinforced by the Pembrokeshire tradition which is the basis of Waldo Williams' poem '*Llandysilio-yn-Nyfed*', in which Tysilio is described as an exile from Powys who has preferred giving up his throne to taking up the sword.[30]

3. 'A court soldier and honourable...'

The prototype of the soldier turned hermit-saint was Martin of Tours (316-397), whose Latin biography by Sulpitius Severus was widely circulated and very influential in both Wales and Ireland.[31] A Welsh life of Martin, drawn from the writings of Sulpitius and Gregory of Tours, survives and is attributed to Siôn Trevor, Bishop of St Asaph (d. 1410), though it seems to be based on a very much earlier version.[32] Martin had been forcibly enrolled in the Roman army at the age of fifteen. Five years later, in the depths of a freezing winter, he cut his military cloak in half and shared it with a poor man who was in danger of freezing to death. The following night while Martin was asleep he had a vision of Christ wearing the part of the cloak which he had given to the poor stranger. As a result of this Martin decided to be baptized.[33]

He remained in the army until the mid 350s, seeking his discharge from the anti-Christian Emperor Julian the Apostate:

[Martin] said to Caesar, ''Hitherto I have served you as a soldier: allow me now to become a soldier to God.....I am the soldier of Christ: it is not lawful for me to fight.''[34]

Having spent some time with Hilary (Ilar), Bishop of Poitiers, Martin became a hermit, first in Milan and then on the island of Gallinaria. In 361 he founded a religious community at Ligugé. Ten years later the people of Tours kidnapped him in order to make him their bishop, an office which he held for the rest of his life.

Martin's example offered a pattern for other Christian warriors who decided to lay down their arms and become 'soldiers of Christ' engaged in the spiritual warfare of the ascetic life. One such figure may have been Illtud Farchog ('Illtud the Knight'). There is a twelfth century biography of Illtud, apparently composed by a monk of Llanilltud Fawr (Llantwit Major). Canon Doble dismisses the work as being 'of no historical value.'[35] Nevertheless there may be some significance in the portrayal of Illtud as a soldier who became a hermit, following the same pattern as Martin and Pedrog (and probably Tysilio as well).

The life, which was to inspire a *cywydd* by the sixteenth-century Glamorgan poet Lewys Morgannwg, states that Illtud's parents 'vowed to dedicate him to literature.' It was, the author claims, Illtud himself who 'laid aside the study of literature, applying himself to military training, not forgetting however, through any negligence, anything which he had learnt . . . None was more eloquent throughout Gaul than Illtud, the soldier, in discoursing philosophic eloquence.'[36] This paragon left his native Brittany and went to visit the court of his cousin, king Arthur. From there, 'accompanied by his very honourable wife, Trynihid,' he moved on to the court of 'Poulentus, king of the Glamorgan folk':

> The king, perceiving that he was a court soldier and honourable retained him with much affection, loving him before all of his household and rewarding him bounteously. So he remained with very great honour until he merited to be chosen and preside over the royal household. He ruled the household without any strife, a peaceful governor and second from his master. Gospel precepts were stored (or hidden) in the soldier's breast; incessantly he strove to recount them to those keeping them. The things recounted directed the hearers to perfect works; the perfect works raised those who fulfilled them to a heavenly reward. A soldier he was outwardly in soldier's dress, but inwardly the wisest of British-born. Where-fore he was by king Poulentus made master of the soldiers for his very fine fluency and incomparable mind.[37]

Illtud's biographer portrays him as the incarnation of a twelfth century chivalric-monastic ideal: a combination of courtier, scholar and soldier that reminds a modern reader of Elizabethan figures like Sir Philip Sidney and Sir Walter Raleigh. It is a portrait which owes much to the imagination and little to reality.

The turning point in Illtud's career came when Poulentus' household went out hunting and unlawfully demanded food from St Cadog. They sat down to enjoy their forcibly obtained picnic, but before they had a chance to taste it the earth opened up and swallowed them, 'on account of the unlawful demand and sacrilegious offence.'[38] Illtud, who had disagreed with the company's treatment of Cadog, was fortunately away from the rest of them, indulging in a spot of falconry, when this disaster happened. He was so shaken by the event however, that he went to Cadog, confessed his past faults, and agreed to give up the military life and to become a monk instead.

Baring Gould and Fisher, identifying Poulentus with the Glamorgan chieftain Paul of Penychen, suggest a factual basis for this part of Illtud's biography:

> Illtyd, who at the time was in the service of Paul of Penychen, was hunting, when some of his party got engulfed in a morass and

perished. This so affected the mind of Illtyd that he resolved on renouncing the world.[39]

It does indeed seem that there must have been some sort of crisis in Illtud's life to transform him from '*Illtud Farchog*' ('Illtud the Knight') into the peaceful hermit of Hodnant who gained the reputation of being 'the first great Teacher of Saints in Wales.'[40] The change itself is indicative of the questioning of heroic models and values that is also evident in the story of Pedrog and the Llywarch Hen poems.

The specifically Christian warrior (as opposed to the warrior who happens to be a Christian) seems to have little place in early Welsh Christianity. The only exception is the historically problematic figure of Arthur. Nennius says of the battle of Guinnion fort, 'in it Arthur carried the image of the holy Mary, the everlasting Virgin, on his [shield,] and the heathen were put to flight on that day, and there was a great slaughter upon them, through the power of Our Lord Jesus Christ and the power of the Holy Virgin Mary, his mother.'[41] In the Welsh Annals there is a similar description of the British leader at 'The Battle of Badon, in which Arthur carried the Cross of our Lord Jesus Christ on his shoulders [i.e. *shield*] and the Britons were the victors.'[42] Here Arthur is being presented in the same mould as the Soldier Saints who feature in the liturgy of the embattled Armenian Church:

> Wonderful among the company of martyrs,
> Partakers in the sufferings of Christ,
> Valiant in the contest of battles
> They took the cross of Jesus up on their shoulders.[43]

Such an explicitly militant and militarist view of Christianity runs counter to one of the strongest strands in the Welsh spiritual tradition, despite the '*gwrol ryfelwyr*' ('valiant warriors') who still have a prominent place in the Welsh National Anthem.

Pacifism has become an important element in the mainstream of Welsh nonconformity, particularly during the present century. In his recent history of Christian pacifism in Wales Dr Gwynfor Evans traces its beginnings to the Welsh Quakers of the mid-seventeenth century, although he does refer to Illtud and to earlier figures like Martin of Tours, Vitricius and Paulinus of Nola.[44] It does however seem possible that the growing Welsh tendency to link pacifism and Christianity, the most powerful modern exponent of which has been the Quaker poet Waldo Williams, has its roots in the criticism of heroic attitudes which began to develop in the Celtic Church in Wales.

The heroic poetry of the *Gododdin*, with its catalogue of young men killed and lives wasted, was bound to create a backlash among Christians who valued martyrdom for the faith but increasingly questioned the worth of 'futile battles'. Even the imaginary picture of 'A court soldier, and honourable', like the Illtud portrayed by his medieval biographer, could not survive the test of war's brutal realities. In our century the same questions which troubled their forebears have surfaced in the minds of Welsh and Anglo-Welsh poets and writers. David Jones' *In Parenthesis*, describing the poet's experiences in the trenches and drawing on the *Gododdin* and other areas of early Welsh tradition in the process, includes, as its epigraph, the description of Heilyn's disastrous opening of the door that destroyed the paradise of forgetfulness in the *Mabinogi* of Branwen.[45] While Lewis Valentine, later to become one of the greatest Welsh Baptist preachers, wrote a heart-felt cry in his diary from the trenches of Flanders, which echoes the protests of Pedrog and the other early Welsh Christian soldiers who shattered their spears in the hope of ending the hideous inhumanity of war:

Beth pe gwyddai mamau Cymru, a mamau pob gwlad yn wir, fel y dirdynnir ac y rhwygir eu plant! A'r Duw mawr, i beth![46]

('What if the mothers of Wales, and indeed the mothers of every country, knew how their children are tortured and torn to pieces! And great God, for what purpose!')

NOTES

[1] *Llywelyn y Beirdd,* edited by J.E. Caerwyn Williams, Eurys Rolant and Alan Llwyd ([Caernarfon], 1984), p.97.

[2] Brynley F. Roberts, '*Culhwch ac Olwen,* The Triads, Saints' Lives' in *The Arthur of the Welsh: The Arthurian Legend in Medieval Welsh Literature,* edited by Rachel Bromwich, A.O.H. Jarman and Brynley F. Roberts (Cardiff, 1991), p.85.

[3] Nennius, *British History and The Welsh Annals,* edited and translated by John Morris (London, 1980), p.45.

[4] Thomas Charles-Edwards, 'The Arthur of History' in *The Arthur of the Welsh,* p.29.

[5] Roberts, '*Culhwch ac Olwen*', p.81; see also *Trioedd Ynys Prydein,* pp.160-2; *Culhwch ac Olwen,* edited by Rachel Bromwich and D. Simon Evans (Cardiff, 1988), p.lxxxii.

[6] Gildas, *The Ruin of Britain,* p.28.

[7] *Trioedd Ynys Prydein,* pp.206-10.

[8] *Trioedd Ynys Prydein,* pp.59-60.

[9] *Trioedd Ynys Prydein,* pp.252-3.

[10] Baring Gould and Fisher, *Lives,* IV, 94.

[11] Baring Gould and Fisher, *Lives,* IV, 97-9.

[12] Baring Gould and Fisher, *Lives,* IV, 95, attempt to reconcile the two versions.

[13] Elissa Henken, *The Welsh Saints: A Study in Patterned Lives* (Cambridge, 1991), p.27; see also Henken, *Traditions of the Welsh Saints,* pp.200-1.

[14] Baring Gould and Fisher, *Lives,* IV, 102-3.

[15] *Gwaith Lewis Glyn Cothi,* edited by John Jones and Walter Davies (Oxford, 1837), p.216.

[16] *The Poetical Works of Dafydd Nanmor,* edited by Thomas Roberts and Ifor Williams (Cardiff, 1923), p.15.

[17] *Trioedd Ynys Prydein,* p.493.

[18] *The Poems of Taliesin,* edited by Sir Ifor Williams (Dublin, 1968), p.7.

[19] Nora Chadwick, *The British Heroic Age* (Cardiff, 1976), p.70.

[20] Kenneth Hurlstone Jackson, *The Gododdin: The Oldest Scottish Poem* (Edinburgh, 1969), p.26.

[21] Ifor Williams, *Canu Aneurin* (Cardiff, 1970), p.3.

[22] Jenny Rowland, *Early Welsh Saga Poetry* (Cambridge, 1990), p.19.

[23] Ifor Williams, *Canu Llywarch Hen* (Cardiff, 1970), p.5. *'vygcot'* is probably an error in the transmission of the text. See Williams, *Canu Llywarch Hen,* p.82; Rowland, *Early Welsh Saga Poetry,* p.524.

[24] Sir Ifor Williams, *Lectures on Early Welsh Poetry* (Dublin, 1970), p.41.

[25] Kenneth Jackson, Early Welsh Gnomic Poems (Cardiff, 1973), p.20.

[26] Thomas Gwynn Jones, *Y Dwymyn 1934-5* (Cardiff, 1972), p.34.

[27] Baring Gould and Fisher, *Lives,* IV, 296-300.

[28] *Hen Gerddi Crefyddol,* edited by Henry Lewis (Cardiff, 1931), pp.36, 118.

[29] Henken, *Traditions of the Welsh Saints,* p.272.

[30] *Cerddi Waldo Williams,* edited by J.E. Caerwyn Williams (Gregynog, 1992), p.102.

[31] Christopher Donaldson, *Martin of Tours: Parish Priest, Mystic and Exorcist* (London, 1985), p.141.

[32] *Buchedd Sant Martin,* edited by Evan John Jones (Cardiff, 1945), pp.v-vi.

[33] Sulpitius Severus, *The Life of St Martin* in *A Select Library of the Nicene and Post-Nicene Fathers of the Christian Church,* second series, edited by Philip Schaff and Henry Wace (Grand Rapids, 1982), XI, 5.

[34] Sulpitius, *Life of St Martin,* p.6.

[35] G.H. Doble, *Lives of the Welsh Saints,* edited by D. Simon Evans (Cardiff, 1971), p.136.

[36] A.W. Wade-Evans, *Vitae Sanctorum Britanniae et Genealogiae* (Cardiff, 1944), pp.195, 197.

[37] Wade-Evans, *Vitae,* p.197.

[38] Wade-Evans, *Vitae,* p.197.

[39] Baring Gould and Fisher, *Lives,* III, 306.

[40] Baring Gould and Fisher, *Lives,* III, 309.

[41] Nennius, *British History,* p.35.

[42] Nennius, *British History,* p.45.

[43] *Divine Liturgy of the Armenian Apostolic Orthodox Church,* translated by Tiran Abp. Nersoyan (London, 1984), p.180.

[44] Gwynfor Evans, *Heddychiaeth Gristnogol yng Nghymru* (Llandysul, 1991), pp.3-5.

[45] David Jones, *In Parenthesis* (London, 1969), p.[xix].

[46] Lewis Valentine, *Dyddiadur Milwr a Gweithiau Eraill,* edited by John Emyr (Llandysul, 1988), p.46.

PART TWO: THE LANGUAGE OF CREATION

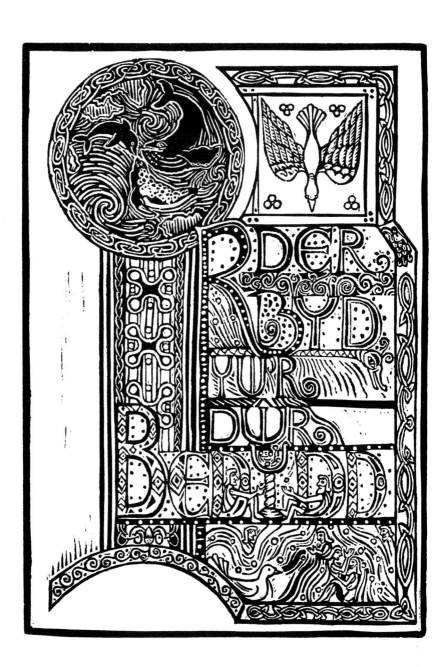

Chapter Four:

AMONG THE BIRDS AND ANIMALS

1. 'He made wild beasts tame...'

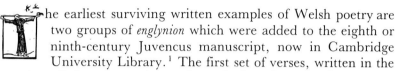he earliest surviving written examples of Welsh poetry are two groups of *englynion* which were added to the eighth or ninth-century Juvencus manuscript, now in Cambridge University Library.[1] The first set of verses, written in the margins of the manuscript and nearly lost forever when it was trimmed by an over-zealous binder, reflects the grim and dislocated world of Welsh society following the collapse of Britain. Sir Ifor Williams comments:

> The speaker is evidently a chief; very much on his dignity, or else very low-spirited. He has lost all his war-band, or retinue, in battle probably, except one foreign mercenary, whom he calls his Frank. His hall this night is empty, desolate. Instead of a merry host of noble youths to share the feast, there are only left the Chief himself and this one hireling. His heart is bitter within him. He cannot sing, laugh, jest, however much he may drink of the clear mead. His mood is far from merriment of any sort. He looks at his sole companion, this hired soldier—and loathes the sight of him.[2]

This bleak little poem echoes the despair and disillusionment that set in as the Britons began to realize that so much of their former territory was lost forever. The old heroic rhetoric evaporated in the face of the reality of defeat and loss.

The second group of *englynion,* inscribed on the first page of the manuscript sometime during the tenth century, are completely different in tone and subject. The language is archaic and obscure, and not all the poem is legible, but Sir Ifor Williams translates the opening stanzas as follows:

> Almighty Creator, thou hast made...
>
> The world cannot express in song bright and melodious, even though the grass and the trees should sing, all thy glories (miracles, riches), O true Lord!

The Father has wrought [such a multitude] of wonders in this world that it is difficult to find an equal number. Letters cannot contain it, letters cannot express it.

Jesus wrought on behalf of the hosts of Christendom [such a multitude] of miracles when he came (? like grass is the number of them).

He who made the wonder of the world, will save us, has saved us. It is not too great toil to praise the Trinity.[3]

The contrast between the two poems is striking. There is no trace in the second group of *englynion* of the pessimism and despair which had marked the earlier verses. Instead the poet glories in the natural world and its divine Creator. Emptiness and bitterness are replaced by exuberance and '*gorfoleddu*' (ecstatic rejoicing): 'He who made the wonder of the world, will save us, has saved us'—and therefore hope is restored.

The source of this rebirth of hope lies in the ascetic movement's experience of the natural world. The Egyptian desert fathers had sought to escape from the 'world' in the sense of a corrupt church and society. They discovered a very different sort of world in the desert to which they fled, and developed an affirmative approach to God's creation which balanced the rigour of their own ascetic practices. Derwas Chitty notes that:

> ...the saints themselves...had...a positive love for the stark beauty of their wildernesses. Antony was to compare a monk out of the desert to a fish out of water. And when a philosopher asked him how he could endure without books his long solitude, he would point to the mountainous wilderness around him: 'My book, O philosopher, is the nature of created things, and it is present when I will, for me to read the words of God.'[4]

The desert hermits combined this appreciation of their natural environment with a close and harmonious relationship with many of the creatures which inhabited it. Sulpitius Severus, the disciple and biographer of Martin of Tours, brought this aspect of their life to the attention of Western Christians in his *Dialogue Concerning the Virtues of the Monks of the East*. The *Dialogue* contains a description of a visit to the desert monks by Sulpitius' friend Postumianus. One hermit had a tame lion, whom he calmly fed with dates, much to the astonishment of his terrified Gallic guest. Another monk regularly fed a she-wolf, which showed penitence after stealing bread from him.[5] Such stories helped to develop the idea that the ascetics were somehow recreating the idyllic state of Paradise before Adam's fall: 'the purity of the holy man restoring the harmony and goodness of original creation.'[6]

The ascetics of the Celtic lands, following in the Egyptian tradition, similarly developed a positive attitude towards the wild creatures with whom they shared the cliff-sides, forests and islands where they settled. This may partly have been the result of their way of life itself, as Roger Sorrell suggests:

> ...who now can imagine the joy and new sense of security the frightened and lonely ascetic would have felt at the approach of curious and perhaps even friendly wild animals (as they sometimes are when never previously confronted by humans)?[7]

This view would seem to be reinforced by the experience of more recent hermits. The Russian staretz Seraphim of Sarov (1759-1833) befriended (or was befriended by) a bear during his period of solitude in the depths of the forest, while Thomas Merton in his hermitage in Kentucky in the 1960s remarked on the fearlessness of the deer who came to graze nearby.[8] Merton mentions that he was reading Kenneth Jackson's *Early Celtic Nature Poetry* at that time.[9] Reflecting on the nature poetry of the Irish ascetics, Jackson wrote:

> ...the ultimate significance of the hermit's relationship with nature is something that transcends both nature and hermit alike. The woodland birds might sing to him around his cell, but through it all, rarely expressed, always implicit, is the understanding that the bird and hermit are joining together in an act of worship; to him the very existence of nature was a song of praise in which he himself took part by entering into harmony with nature . . . It was from this harmony with nature, this all-perceiving contemplation of it, that the Irish hermits reached to a more perfect unison with God.[10]

Several of those Irish hermits made their way across the sea to Wales. Perhaps the most notable of them was Brynach, who settled at Nevern in Pembrokeshire in the sixth century. His biography was written by someone from that area six centuries later.[11] The author portrays Brynach's life as ascetic in the extreme:

> He wasted his body with continual fastings, and reduced it with frequent vigils. He checked the insolence of the flesh with the

roughness of his garments, and in the chilliness of cold water which he entered daily. What he withdrew from his mouth, what from his hand, what from his whole body, he converted to the use of the poor. If he could acquire any thing, he reserved it to relieve their need. He was incessantly engaged in prayers, save when he was refreshing his body with food or sleep.[12]

This rigorous regime so sanctified Brynach that, according to his biographer, he frequently met and talked with angels on the mountain between Nevern and Newport, which as a result became known as Carn Ingli ('The Mount of Angels').

The supernatural side of Brynach's existence is, however, balanced by a picture of his involvement with the natural world, including some unintentionally comic details:

> . . . he made wild beasts tame at his bidding, their savage way of life being laid aside. Therefore, if he ever wished to go from abode to abode, he called up from a herd the two stags which he desired to draw the car, wherein the furniture to be carried away was placed. When loosed from the yoke, they returned to their wonted pastures. Also, a Cow, which he had segregated from the others, as if unique and singular for his need, both on account of the size of her body, because she was larger than the rest, and also on account of the abundance of her milk, he deputed to the custody of a Wolf, which in the manner of a well-trained herdsman drove the Cow in the morning to the pastures, and in the evening brought her home in safety.[13]

Despite the imaginative embroidery, the underlying idea of the hermit's harmonious relationship with the creatures around his cell is clear. Local tradition relates that Brynach was able to speak with the birds, a notion that may stem from his association with the cuckoo, which is always supposed to arrive in Nevern on the seventh of April, St Brynach's Day.[14] The Pembrokeshire hermit emerges from the folk-memories of him as a man at peace with both the natural and the supernatural world, his wholeness of vision apparently characteristic of the spiritual movement of which he was a part.

2. 'To give safety to this little wild hare...'

In the surviving traditions about ascetics in Wales the harmony symbolized by their relationship with both the domesticated and wild animals that surrounded them is repeatedly portrayed as being under threat. The hermits had turned their back on the 'world', in the sense of organized human society, but that did not prevent that same 'world' from breaking into their lives and attempting to disrupt or destroy their private attempts to recreate paradise. Govan, as we have seen, was attacked by pirates on the cliffs of Pembrokeshire. Brynach comes into confrontation with Maelgwn of Gwynedd when the latter steals the saint's favourite cow and decides to kill and cook it. Maelgwn also clashed with Cybi, who refused to let him have a wild goat which had run to the saint for protection. [15]

These conflicts most commonly occur between hermits and hunters, usually kings or princes. The ascetics give refuge and sanctuary to hunted animals, thus normally incurring the wrath of those who are pursuing them. The arguments seem to reflect two different views of humanity's place in creation. For the hermits humankind and the animals are interdependent and should live in harmony together. For the hunters man is lord of creation, free to use the animals in whatever way he wishes. The clash may also be between a rigidly hierarchical view of human society (the huntsmen are almost always portrayed as men of authority and power) and a much more egalitarian approach espoused by the ascetics, to whom all men and women have value and potential, being made in the image and likeness of God. These differing social views reflected different attitudes towards the natural world as well.

One of the most famous examples of this type of conflict is the story of Melangell (Monacella) and the hare, derived from a fairly late manuscript. [16] Melangell is said to have been the daughter of an Irish King. She apparently took a vow of celibacy and, in order to avoid being married off to an Irish nobleman, fled to Wales, where she settled as a hermit at Pennant in Powys. The *Historia Monacellae* records that in the year 604 Brochwel Ysgithrog, Prince of Powys, decided to go hunting at Pennant:

> ...when the hounds of the same prince had started a hare, the dogs were following the hare and he was pursuing to a certain bramble thicket, a thicket large and thorny; in which thicket he found a certain virgin, beautiful in appearance, praying as devoutly as

possible, and given up to divine contemplation, together with the said hare lying under the extremity or fold of her garments (with its face turned towards the dogs) boldly and intrepidly. Then the prince vociferating "Catch her, little dogs! catch her!" the more he shouted while he urged them on, the more remotely and further off did the dogs retreat, and fled from the little wild animal howling.[17]

The prince was astonished at this, and asked the beautiful young woman who she was.

Melangell told him her story, and Brochwel was so impressed that he exclaimed:

> "O most worthy virgin Monacella, I find that thou art a handmaiden of the true God, and a most sincere worshipper of Christ; wherefore because it has pleased the supreme and almighty God, for thy merits, to give safety to this little wild hare, with safe conduct and protection from the attack and pursuit of the ravenous and biting dogs, I give and present to thee, with a most willing mind, these my lands for the service of God, and that they may be a perpetual asylum, refuge and defence, in honour of thy name, O excellent virgin . . ."[18]

Pennant Melangell thus became a place of sanctuary for human fugitives, in recognition of Melangell's rescue of the hunted hare. The saint herself remained there in solitude for the next thirty-seven years, 'And the hares, wild little animals, just the same as . . . tame animals, were in a state of familiarity about her every day throughout her whole life.'[19]

A carved wooden screen illustrating Melangell's story was put in the church at Pennant in medieval times. It includes the figure of Brochwel, Melangell, the hare, a greyhound and another dog, and Brochwel's unfortunate huntsman who, it is said, raised his horn to his lips, only to find that it got stuck to them.[20] Baring Gould and Fisher note that Melangell became the patron saint of hares, which were thereafter called '*Ŵyn Melangell*' ('Melangell's lambs') by the people of the area. No one in Pennant Melangell parish would ever kill a hare, and if any one saw a hare being hunted and shouted out '*Duw a Melangell a'th gadwo!*' ('God and Melangell preserve you!') the hare would always escape.[21]

In recent years Melangell has become seen as the patron saint of animals and nature in Wales, with the setting up of a society, '*Cymdeithas Melangell*', in her memory. Its aims include a concern for

66

animal welfare, conservation and the natural world.[22] Melangell's story has also inspired a song by Desmond Healy, which has been recorded by the Powys folk group Plethyn:

A glywsoch chi yr hanes am sgwarnog fach y ffridd
Yn rhedeg i ffedog Melangell 'slawer dydd,
A chael gan y Santes, rhag helfa'r t'ywysog cas
Ei rhyddid i redeg yn rhydd drwy'r borfa las.

I'r sgwarnog a'r llwynog, y cudyll coch a'i gyw,
Rhown ninnau bob nodded, fe'u ganed hwythau i fyw.
Y ffwlbart a'r wenci, a'r dwrgi draw'n y llyn,
Boed iddynt oll eu rhyddid ar ddôl a phant a bryn.[23]

('Have you heard the story about the little hillside hare running into Melangell's apron long ago and receiving from the saint her freedom from the wicked prince's hunt, to run freely through the green grass. To the hare and the fox, the kestrel and its chick, we give every protection, they were born to live. May the polecat, the weasel and the otter over in the lake all have their freedom in meadow, valley and hill.')

It might be tempting to dismiss the attitudes expressed in Healy's *'Cân Melangell'* as reflecting a late twentieth-century urban and suburban sentimentality towards animals. However it is worth recalling the pictures of a harmonious relationship with nature contained in the Irish monastic poetry of the ninth century, which apparently is the fruit of very similar ideas and ideals. One notable example is the poem in which Marbán the hermit defends his way of life to his half-brother Guaire, king of Connacht, describing the many different creatures who visit his hut:

> Tame pigs and goats
> and baby pigs
>   at home all round it,
> and wild pigs also,
> tall deer and their does,
>   badgers and their brood.
>
> In peaceful parties
> crowds from the country
>   visit my home:

67

foxes gather
in the woods before it
and that is lovely.
. . . .

The music of pigeons
in their glossy throats
   makes lovely stir,
and the murmur of thrushes
sweet and homely
   over my house;

beetles, bees,
with their tiny buzzing
   and delicate hum;
wild barnacle geese
(it will soon be Samain!)
   with their wild dark music;

The busy linnet,
brown restless spirit
   on the hazel bough,
and then woodpeckers,
speckle-hooded,
   in enormous flights;

they come, the white ones,
gulls and herons,
   till the harbour echoes
and (no sad music)
the brown hen fowl
   in the russet heather. [24]

J. E. Caerwyn Williams notes the way in which Irish poets of the ninth
and following centuries 'put poems which talk about the joy and
pleasures of life in the open almost without exception in the mouth of
some early monk or hermit like Colum-cille, Mo-ling, Manchán,
Ceallach or Marbán.' He comments that this 'gives the impression
that nature poetry was connected in the minds of those poets with
different monks and hermits in the sixth and seventh centuries.' He
agrees with Professor Gerard Murphy that the impulse behind this

poetry is essentially Christian, stemming from a belief in God as creator of everything combined with the monastic experience of life in solitary places.[25] Myles Dillon echoes this view:

> ...the spirit of the early Franciscans was, in a measure, anticipated in Ireland. It seems that this awareness of the whole of creation as the work of God—a delight in the forms and sounds which are an occasion for praising and thanking the Providence which gave them—is the source of much of the nature poetry.[26]

Irish hermits in Wales, like Melangell and Brynach, reflected this rediscovery of the wholeness of creation, which also left its mark on the Welsh spiritual tradition.

3. 'The protection and favour of the Creator...'

The Welsh and Irish ascetics had a model who antedated even St Paul the Hermit and St Antony of Egypt. Mark's description of Jesus' sojourn in the desert could have been applied to Brynach and many other solitaries (though their self-imposed period of isolation was longer): 'And he was in the wilderness forty days, tempted by Satan; and he was with the wild beasts; and the angels ministered to him.'[27] The hermits, like Jesus himself, were involved in spiritual warfare in their lonely huts and cells. For them, as for Jesus (or so Mark seems to imply), the wild beasts became allies in this struggle, helping them to become aware of God's love enfolding his creation.[28]

In his remarkable poem 'Crist Natur' ('The Christ of Nature') the modern Cardiganshire poet Donald Evans has restated Christ's view of the natural world as it emerges from the Gospels:

Carai gymeriad adar, yr haid a ymddiriedai'n Ei Dad;
Carai ŵyn, y cywreiniaf: yr ŵyn, y diniweitiaf eu natur.

Carai fwystfilod y cyrion: y rhai a drigiannai'n y gwyllt;
Carai'u dibyniad cadarn ar yr hyn a gyfrannai yr anial.

Carai wenith yn crynu wrth bendrymu'n felyn gan faeth;
Carai'r mynydd-dir caerog, yr anghyfannedd lle tyfai heddwch.

Carai'r ddaear, ei charu fel câr, am mai daear Duw yw hi;
Carai hi, gan y'i crewyd gan Ei Dad o'r dim yn deml i Fywyd.[29]

69

('He loved the character of birds, the flock that trusted in His Father; He loved lambs, the most skilfully made: lambs with the most innocent nature. He loved the beasts of the margin-lands: those that dwelt in the wild; He loved their staunch dependence on that which the desert could give. He loved the wheat swaying, weighed down with yellow nourishment; He loved the mountain fastnesses, the uninhabited places where peace grew. He loved the earth, loved her like a relative because she is God's earth; He loved her because she was created by His Father out of nothing as a temple for Life.')

Such a positive and protective view of God's creation is seen both by the modern Welsh poet and the Celtic hermits of the sixth and seventh centuries as quintessentially Christian. It drew additional strength, however, from elements in pre-Christian culture and religion in the Celtic lands.

Beuno was a holy man who probably died around the year 642.[30] His cult was widespread in north Wales and he became the subject of a great many stories and traditions. Baring Gould and Fisher quote Sir John Rhys' version of one such legend:

When S. Beuno lived at Clynnog, he used to go regularly to preach at Llanddwyn on the opposite side of the water, which he always crossed on foot. But one Sunday he accidentally dropped his book of sermons into the water, and when he had failed to recover it a *gylfin-hir,* or curlew, came by, picked it up, and placed it on a stone out of reach of the tide. The saint prayed for the protection and favour of the Creator for the *gylfin-hir*; it was granted, and so nobody ever knows where that bird makes its nest.[31]

This delightful story began, of course, as an attempt to explain why it was impossible to find a curlew's nest. The bird's ability to hide its nest is seen as a gift from God the Creator, resulting from Beuno's response to the curlew's kindness. The saint is regarded as a protector of nature, just as Melangell was, but something else has been added. According to the story-teller, Beuno's prayer actually changes the natural order by transforming the curlew's nesting habits. The Christian holy man is beginning to acquire some of the characteristics associated with mythological Celtic figures.

The surviving traditions about him do indeed make Beuno out to be somewhat larger-than-life. He is credited with raising either six or seven people from the dead. He had a great reputation for giving huge feasts, apparently miraculously produced from next-to-nothing. Many stories link him with trees. His staff grew bark and sprouted leaves and nuts, turning into a tree. An oak which he planted had a bending branch. Welshmen could pass under it underscathed, whereas any Englishman who ventured beneath it would die immediately. All trees growing on land dedicated to Beuno were regarded as sacred, and it was said that dreadful things would happen to anyone who tried to cut them down. Bullocks, as well as any calves or lambs born with '*nod Beuno*' ('Beuno's mark'—a slit in the ear), were offered up to Beuno at Clynnog, the centre of his cult, even after the Reformation. The proceeds of their sale were put in '*cyff Beuno*', an ancient chest scooped out of the solid trunk of an oak.[32]

The stories which portray Beuno as a giver of feasts and a raiser from the dead may have their origins in the feeding of the five thousand and the raising of Lazarus, being no more than that which the tellers of tales and their audience expected of an exceptionally holy man. The link with trees and bullocks, however, points towards pre-Christian connections. The importance of sacred trees both in pre-Christian Celtic religion and in Celtic Christianity will be touched on in the next chapter. As for the bulls, Miranda Green has noted that

The precise significance of bull-symbolism in the Celtic world is obscure. But the frequency of its iconographic occurrence as an isolated image, and the abundant evidence for ritual and sacrifice suggests that it possessed a sanctity for its own sake. We know from Pliny that white bulls were sacrificed in the Druidic ceremonial of the mistletoe-cutting . . . much of the early Irish vernacular tradition is concerned with magico-divine bulls . . . Bulls were associated also with the selection of kings in Ireland.[33]

One of the most striking Celtic artefacts to have survived from Romano-British Wales is a beautiful ox-head escutcheon, discovered at Welshpool.[34] This may be evidence of a pre-Christian bull cult. It seems probable that bullocks were offered to some local Celtic deity at Clynnog long before Beuno's time, and that the saint eventually not only usurped the god's position, but also took on some of his characteristics in the minds of the people of the area.

The blurring of the borders between the historic and the mythological is one of the characteristics of early Welsh culture. Taliesin, the sturdily historical sixth-century chronicler of Urien Rheged and his son Owain's attempts to stem the Northumbrian invasion, becomes mixed up with a strange shape-changing legendary figure from the

71

area around Bala. Arthur, probably in reality a warrior chief from near Hadrian's Wall, acquires a magic ship and a magic sword and sets sail for an island where the cauldron of the otherworld is kept in a fortress of glass. The mythical Taliesin joins him on this unearthly expedition. The stories of saints were as much the subject of this type of imaginative confusion and elaboration as were the sagas about poets and warriors. The traditions which have clustered around Beuno contain obvious examples of the results of this process. Some of them, like the echoes of ancient bull sacrifices lingering on in the Wales of Elizabeth I, are strange and rather repellent. But occasionally, within this intertwining of the real and the unreal, Celtic Christianity makes creative contact with the religious ideas which had preceded it. The result, as in the story of Beuno and the curlew, can sometimes be a fresh and telling insight into the place and responsibility of humanity within creation.

NOTES

[1] Williams, *Beginnings of Welsh Poetry*, pp.89-121, contains an edition of the poems and a discussion of the manuscript.
[2] Williams, *Lectures on Early Welsh Poetry*, p.29.
[3] Williams, *Beginnings of Welsh Poetry*, p.102.
[4] Chitty, *The Desert a City*, p.6.
[5] Sulpitius Severus, *Dialogues* in *A Select Library of the Nicene and Post-Nicene Fathers of the Christian Church*, second series, edited by Philip Schaff and Henry Wace (Grand Rapids, 1982), XI, 30-1.
[6] Roger D. Sorrell, *St. Francis of Assisi and Nature: Tradition and Innovation in Western Christian Attitudes toward the Environment* (New York, 1988), p.20.
[7] Sorrell, *St. Francis of Assisi and Nature*, p.18.
[8] Valentine Zander, *St Seraphim of Sarov* (London, 1975), p.61.
[9] Thomas Merton, *A Vow of Conversation: Journals 1964-1965* (Basingstoke, 1988), pp.207-8, 58.
[10] Kenneth Jackson, *Studies in Early Celtic Nature Poetry* (Cambridge, 1935), pp.108-9.
[11] Wade-Evans, *Vitae*, p.xi.
[12] Wade-Evans, *Vitae*, p.11.
[13] Wade-Evans, *Vitae*, p.11.
[14] Henken, *Traditions of the Welsh Saints*, p.279.
[15] Henken, *The Welsh Saints*, p.33.
[16] A seventeenth century transcription of the manuscript is reproduced in *Archaeologia Cambrensis*, III (1848), pp.139-42.
[17] *Archaeologia Cambrensis*, III, 139-40.
[18] *Archaeologia Cambrensis*, III, 140-1.
[19] *Archaeologia Cambrensis*, III, 141.
[20] A detailed description of the screen is given in *Archaeologia Cambrensis*, III, 225-7.
[21] Baring Gould and Fisher, *Lives*, III, 465.

[22] The aims of *Cymdeithas Melangell* are outlined in the sleeve notes of the 1987 L.P. record 'Byw a Bod' by Plethyn (SAIN 1393M).

[23] Words from Plethyn, 'Byw a Bod' (SAIN 1393M).

[24] *The New Oxford Book of Irish Verse*, edited with translations by Thomas Kinsella (Oxford, 1986), pp.33, 35.

[25] J.E. Caerwyn Williams, *Traddodiad Llenyddol Iwerddon* (Cardiff, 1958), p.72.

[26] Myles Dillon, 'Early Lyric Poetry' in *Early Irish Poetry*, edited by James Carney (Cork, 1969), p.14.

[27] Mark 1. 12 (RSV).

[28] See the comments on Mark's verse by Ian Bradley, *God is Green: Christianity and the Environment* (London, 1990), pp.75-6.

[29] Donald Evans, *Cread Crist* (Caernarfon, 1986), p.23.

[30] *Dictionary of Welsh Biography*, p.642.

[31] Baring Gould and Fisher, *Lives*, I, 220.

[32] Henken, *Traditions of the Welsh Saints, pp.75-86*, Baring Gould and Fisher, *Lives*, I, 217-21.

[33] Miranda Green, *The Gods of the Celts* (Gloucester, 1986), pp.178-9.

[34] Green, *Gods of the Celts*, pp.177, 225.

Chapter Five:

STANDING STONES, SACRED TREES
AND RAIN-MAKING

1. 'The sign of a cross carved on a standing stone.'

n archaeologist recently described standing stones as being 'among the more enigmatic stone monuments,' remarking that 'No convincing explanation can yet be suggested for them, and it is likely that not all had the same function.'[1] What is certain is that many of these stones, which are distributed throughout Western Britain and Ireland, acquired a religious significance, whether or not that was the intention of those who first erected them. Writing of pagan Celtic religion, Anne Ross notes that 'there is much evidence to show that stones themselves, whether decorated in the Celtic manner...or whether merely as blocks of stone or standing stones, were venerated in their own right, and were believed to possess strange powers.'[2] One of the most significant recorded incidents in the development of Celtic Christianity is the encounter between Samson and the worshippers of such a stone.

Samson (c.485-565) is one of the best documented Welsh saints. His biography was probably written in the early seventh century, though its date has been the subject of some scholarly argument.[3] The author claimed that his work was based on very reliable sources:

> ...these words are not put together on the lines of rash surmisings of my own, or those of confused and unauthorised rumours; but on what I derived from a certain religious and venerable old man whose house beyond the sea Samson himself founded. And he, leading a catholic and religious life there, for nearly eighty years, in times most approximate to those of the aforesaid St. Samson, and being himself a cousin of St. Samson and a deacon, truthfully assured me that St. Samson's mother had handed (the information) to his uncle, a most holy deacon, who was himself cousin to St. Samson, and (the old man) kindly related to me many particulars of the saint's wonderful career.[4]

The biographer outlines Samson's life from his birth in Dyfed, through his education by Illtud and his time as a monk on Ynys Bŷr

(Caldey Island), where he succeeded the hapless Pŷr as abbot (the latter had got hopelessly drunk one night and fallen head first into a deep pit on the island, dying shortly afterwards from his injuries). Samson then went on a missionary journey to Ireland, returning to become a hermit in south Pembrokeshire. Having been consecrated as a bishop by Dyfrig, he settled in Cornwall for some years, finally moving across to Brittany, where he ended his days in the famous monastery which he had founded at Dôl.

Samson's encounter with the stone-worshippers occurred during his time in Cornwall. While travelling through the district of Tricurius (Trigg) he came across a group of people enacting some kind of ritual in front of 'an abominable image' on the summit of a hill. Samson 'gently admonished them that they ought not to forsake the one God who created all things and worship an idol.' According to his biographer, the saint clinched his argument with a miracle. A boy had been thrown from a swift horse and was lying, apparently lifeless, on the ground. Samson dismissed the Cornish tribesmen's image as clearly unable to do anything to help the lad, and then told them that "If you promise that you will utterly destroy this idol and no longer adore it, I, with God's assistance, will bring the dead man to life." After two hours of fervent prayer by the Welsh bishop the young horseman recovered completely. A modern reader might suspect that he had been suffering from concussion, but Samson's audience were profoundly impressed, prostrating themselves at the saint's feet and smashing the idol to bits.[5]

What is especially significant about this incident, however, is that Samson did not leave the Cornishmen without a focus for their worship. He replaced the 'abominable image' on 'the summit of a certain hill' with a symbol of his own. His biographer had seen it himself, writing that 'On this hill I myself have been and have adored and with my hand have traced the sign of the cross which St. Samson with his own hand carved by means of an iron instrument on a standing stone.'[6] Samson knew that the tribesmen still needed an object around which to centre their religious rituals. So he turned an ancient sacred stone into a symbol of Christian devotion. The rough cross that he carved may well have resembled the one at Middle Moor, St Breward (Simonward), in the Deanery of Trigg Minor, a picture of which is included in Arthur G. Langdon's *Old Cornish Crosses*. Langdon comments that this particular cross 'is evidently a very old example, and is most rudely executed and somewhat mutilated.'[7]

The tribesmen's rituals may have undergone a similar 'conversion' to that of their sacred stones. Samson's biographer refers to 'men worshipping an idol...by means of a play in honour of an image,' and says that the Cornish tribesmen 'pleaded that it was not wrong to celebrate the mysteries of their progenitors in a play.'[8] The most significant surviving works of Cornish literature are the *Ordinalia* (a fourteenth century trilogy of mystery plays about the creation of the world and the death and resurrection of Christ), *Beunans Meriasek* (a fifteenth century play about the patron saint of Camborne) and *Gwryans an Bys* (another play about the creation of the world, probably dating from the sixteenth century, but written down by William Jordan in 1611).[9] Robert Longsworth writes of the origins of the *Ordinalia*:

> This literary Knossos has, in fact, yielded fewer parallels and borrowings than its miners would like to admit. No dramatic sources have been found. The enigma speaks as darkly as ever.[10]

Perhaps it is not too far-fetched to suggest that the '*gwary myrs*'(miracle plays) which played such an important part in the life and culture of late medieval Cornwall had their distant origins in the Christianization of ancient dramatic rituals like the one which Samson interrupted.

When he chose to carve a cross on the standing stone Samson selected a Christian symbol that was only just beginning to win general acceptance. Charles Thomas notes that the cross 'did not appear in art in Britain until the 5th century and was uncommon until, probably, the mid-6th.'[11] Samson was apparently in Cornwall between 521 and 547. It may be that many of the simple stone crosses there date from the time of his mission. Thomas Taylor certainly believed this to be so.[12] The elaborately carved high crosses which were to be produced in the Celtic lands in succeeding centuries and which have become regarded as among the finest artistic achievements of Celtic Christianity thus have their humble beginnings in the actions of wandering missionaries like Samson, carving stark crosses on standing stones to claim them for Christ and his followers.

Turning a stone into a cross is a very direct way of 'Christianizing' it. Other sacred or unusual stones became incorporated into stories told about particular saints. Elissa Henken lists several of them, including Maen Beuno, which was either Beuno's pulpit or the seat he used when talking to Caswallon's cousin, and Maen Cetti at Cefn-y-bryn in Gower, which David was said to have split in two with a stroke of his sword in order to prove that the stone was not sacred after all. She also refers to some of the stones which were said to represent people petrified for angering or outraging a saint—such as the two thieves who foolishly tried to steal Illtud's pigs and the three women of Dwygyfylchi who upset Seiriol by winnowing corn on a Sunday.[13]

Two stones which did become crosses have traditionally been linked with Samson by another colourful folk legend. *Carreg Samson* (Samson's Stone) is the name given to one of two stone crosses by the porch of Llanbadarn Fawr Church, near Aberystwyth. It is said that the two stones once formed Samson's flail, and that while he was threshing corn at Pen Dinas (the site of an ancient hill-fort on the far side of the valley) the flail broke and one of the stones flew off in the direction of Llanbadarn. Samson lost his temper and threw the other stone after it, which is how they both now come to be standing just outside the church.

Samson's name became linked with many other ancient stones and monuments. There is a second *Carreg Samson* on the mountain near Llanddewi Brefi, and the name is also given to two cromlechs in north Pembrokeshire, while another cromlech there is know as Samson's *'ffust'* (flail). Pentre Ifan, the most famous Pembrokeshire cromlech of all, stands in a field named *Corlan Samson* (Samson's Fold). There are Pembrokeshire tumuli known as *Bedd Samson* (Samson's Grave) and *Bys Samson* (Samson's Finger), not to mention *Marbl Samson* (Samson's Marble), a large boulder associated with a third tumulus.[14]

Perhaps it was inevitable that a saint named Samson would become connected in the popular mind with feats of strength worthy of his Biblical namesake. As well as the Llanbadarn legend there are stories telling of Samson throwing a large stone near Rhosycaerau, and another from the summit of the Frenni Fawr.[15] Brittany also has its Samson stones. There is a leaning menhir at Mont-Dôl which has somehow come to be called 'St Samson's Mitre', while a hollow rock near Tregastel is known as 'St Samson's Bed'.[16]

The habit of connecting strangely shaped or significantly positioned stones with holy men or heroes is not unique to Celtic Christians, though Samson, like Arthur, is associated with a surprisingly large number of them. There is however something very special about the process revealed in the story of Samson and the Cornish standing stone. The saint consciously and deliberately transformed a focus of pre-Christian worship into an object of Christian devotion. Samson's biographer himself traced out and adored the sign of the cross carved on the standing stone and in doing so showed as intense a religious fervour as any pagan tribesman worshipping an 'abominable image'. His action reflected a spirituality that was not afraid to used the material world as a means of coming close to 'the one God who created all things.' By incising crosses on sacred stones Samson and his contemporaries Christianized an ancient cult, and in doing so prepared the way for the remarkable artists who would later produce the great masterpieces of Celtic Christian stonework with their message of creation restored and made whole by the cross of Christ.

2. 'They planted a great grove of fruit-bearing trees...'

rees played an important part in pre-Christian Celtic religion. Miranda Green notes that 'The Celtic word 'nemeton' denoting a sacred grove may be traced in derivative form in Celtic place-names from Britain [Aquae Arnemetiae at Buxton for example] and Spain to Galatia in Asia Minor [Drunemeton]'. She records that 'Later commentaries on Lucan say that the Druids worshipped gods in woods without the use of temples.'[17] Anne Ross also states that 'we must regard trees and woods as amongst the most important of the sacred precincts of the Celts, whether or not they were distinguished by any more sophisticated associated structure.'[18]

A passage describing the planting of a Christian sacred grove occurs, somewhat unexpectedly, in the biography of Teilo included in the *Liber Landavensis,* a twelfth-century manuscript whose compilation stemmed from a dispute between the diocese of Llandaff and the neighbouring dioceses of St Davids and Hereford. Teilo's biographer tells how the saint and a group of companions of both sexes left Wales to escape the 'great death' or 'yellow plague', which devastated the country in 547 according to the *Annales Cambriae.*[19] They fled to Cornwall and then on to Brittany, where they were warmly welcomed by Samson. The biographer records that

> [Teilo] and the aforesaid St. Samson planted a great grove of fruit-bearing trees, to the extent of three miles, that is from Dôl as far as Cai, and these woods are honoured with their names until the present day, for they are called the groves of Teilo and Samson.[20]

The *Liber Landavensis* is a highly partisan work of ecclesiastical propaganda and thus has to be treated rather cautiously. Its outline of Teilo's career is often fanciful in the extreme, but it would appear that this particular incident is based on information supplied by a reliable Breton source. Telo (Teilo) is still regarded as the patron saint of apple-trees in the parish of Landaul in Brittany. During the annual *'pardon'* (local processional pilgrimage) there on the eighteenth of September the children carry apple branches in honour of the saint. [21] It is interesting that Samson should be associated with Teilo in the tradition about the planting of the orchard. Perhaps it represents another aspect of Samson's apparent ability to Christianize pagan cults.

The apple-tree was one of the sacred trees of the Celts in the pre-Christian period. [22] Its significance continued in Welsh folk tradition well into modern times. Apples were a symbol of fertility. In early nineteenth-century Glamorgan childless married couples were still occasionally pelted with them. [23] In Cydweli an artificial *'perllan'* (orchard) was carried around the houses at New Year. It is described as

A small rectangular board with a circle marked in the centre and ribs of wood running from the centre to each of the four angles. At each corner of the board an apple was fixed, and within the circle a tree with a miniature bird thereon. [24]

A similar kind of object (with dead wrens in the middle instead of the artificial bird) is referred to in a song published in Carmarthen in 1823, which stems from the Boxing Day ritual of *'hela'r dryw'* (hunting the wren).

> *Mae gennym elor hynod, a drywod dan y llen,*
> *A pherllan wych o afalau yn gyplau uwch ei phen...* [25]

('We have a remarkable bier, and wrens under the curtain, and a splendid orchard of apples in couples above it.')

Apples also played a part in the custom of *'hel calennig'* (collecting New Year's gifts). Originally this was done by adult men, but in most rural Welsh-speaking areas where it has survived only children now tend to take part, though in my own village of Brechfa some of the men still go round singing in search of a *calennig* after midnight on New Year's Eve. What has vanished completely is the *'rhodd calennig'* traditionally carried by the singers. Rhiannon Ifans describes this as

an apple or orange set on three legs made from hazel twigs, which formed a three-legged chair, the legs of which were sometimes carved in patterns. The side of the apple was pierced with another stick as a handle for it all. On the skin of the apple were dried ears of oats or barley, and a sprig of holly, mistletoe, box or rosemary on top of the fruit. Hazelnuts cut in half were put on these leaves, and oats and raisins here and there on the sides of the fruit. The whole thing was covered with white flour. [26]

Dr Ifans says that this object was originally made as a gift to the gods to ensure fruitfulness during the coming year. [27] It was thus part of a fertility rite, as no doubt were the artificial 'orchards' in Cydweli and elsewhere.

The survival of such customs into the nineteenth century is an indication of how deep-rooted the apple and the orchard were as Welsh fertility symbols. The apple also had Christian connotations, being connected with the idea of a lost Eden and the possibility that that Eden might be regained. *Llyfr Du Caerfyrddin* contains verses known as *'Afallennau Myrddin'* ('Myrddin's apple-trees'), referring to the legend of Myrddin (Merlin). A.O.H. Jarman dates the oldest of them to the ninth or tenth centuries. [28] They tell how Myrddin had been hiding for fifty years in the forest of Celyddon after the disastrous battle of Arfderydd in which his lord Gwenddolau had been slain and he himself had killed Gwenddydd's son, before going mad. The *'afallen peren'* ('sweet apple-tree') to which Myrddin repeatedly addresses his lament provides him with a hiding-place but also reminds him of his lost happiness. The echo of Eden seems deliberate, especially in the light of Myrddin's desperate prayer:

> *Guydi porthi heint a hoed am gylch coed Keliton.*
> *Buyf guas guinwydic. gan guledic gorchortion.* [29]

('Having suffered sickness and longing around the wood of Celyddon, may I be a blessed servant of the Lord of Hosts.')

By planting an orchard Teilo and Samson were in effect symbolically recreating Eden, as well as showing that the fruitfulness and fertility so important to pre-Christian Celtic religion also had a significant place in the Christian view of the nature of God's creation. A continuation of this attitude is sometimes seen in some of the woodland love poems of the great fourteenth-century Welsh poet Dafydd ap Gwilym. Thus one scholar has recently commented on them:

> the emphasis is on the spiritual harmony which the poet receives in the woodland setting rather than on the courtly nature of his love. The function of these poems is to convey the need for spiritual

commitment in love, as well as physical desire. By appropriating God's creations to pursue physical love, the poet achieves the necessary synthesis of the sensual and the spiritual.[30]

The poem most commonly cited as an example of this synthesis is *'Offeren y Llwyn'* ('The Mass of the Grove'), which describes a service in a birch grove at which the thrush, a *'llatai'* (love-messenger) from Dafydd's girlfriend Morfudd, acts as the priest:

> *Nid oedd yna, myn Duw mawr,*
> *Ond aur oll yn do'r allawr.*
> *Mi a glywwn mewn gloywiaith*
> *Ddatganu, nid methu, maith,*
> *Darllain i'r plwyf, nid rhwyf rhus,*
> *Efengyl yn ddifyngus.*
> *Codi ar y fryn ynn yna*
> *Afrlladen o ddeilen dda.*
> *Ac eos gain fain fangaw*
> *O gwr y llwyn gar ei llaw,*
> *Clerwraig nant, i gant a gân*
> *Cloch aberth, clau ei chwiban,*
> *A dyrchafel yr aberth*
> *Hyd y nen uwchben y berth;*
> *A chrefydd i'n Dofydd Dad,*
> *A charegl nwyf a chariad.*
> *Bodlon wyf i'r ganiadaeth,*
> *Bedwlwyn o'r coed mwyn a'i maeth.*[31]

('By great God, there was only pure gold around the altar. I heard a lengthy chant that did not falter. The Gospel read clearly to the people of the parish, without stammering or stumbling. Then a wafer of a good leaf was elevated on a hill for our sake. And a beautiful slender eloquent nightingale, the poetess of the valley, sings to a host from the edge of the grove near to us, with her swift whistle, the sacrificial bell, and the sacrifice is raised to heaven above the hedge; and worship to our Lord and Father, and a chalice of (sexual) passion and love. I am content with the music: of all the lovely trees it was the birch grove which nurtured it.')

The ambiguity and tongue-in-cheek quality of Dafydd's poem is only too clear. As R. Geraint Gruffydd has pointed out the poem reflects a conflict rather than a synthesis. He describes it as the clearest expression of the contrast which Dafydd ap Gwilym sees between the church of the grove and the parish church, that is between nature where instinct rules and the human world which is subject to all sorts of rules and conventions. . . . Dafydd prefers the church of the grove to the parish church, and he exalts his chosen church in the *cywydd*.[32]

The fusion of the natural and the spiritual which Teilo and Samson seem to have attempted had broken down as a result of the rigidity and corruption of some aspects of medieval religion. Dafydd may well have been seeking to reunite the two, though it seems more likely that his main aim was to show up the inadequacy of the mean-spirited clergy who were so often the targets of his satire. Gruffydd suggests that Dafydd's *cywydd* may have been influenced by a similar French poem.[33] Nevertheless the birch grove itself has a distinctively Welsh atmosphere to it, the birch tree being, like the apple-tree, connected in Welsh tradition with fertility. The Welsh equivalent of the English maypole was known as *'bedwen haf'* ('a summer birch'), *'bedwen Ifan'* ('John's birch') or *'bedwen Fai'* ('a May birch').[34] Dafydd's *'Bedwlwyn o'r coed mwyn'* is a descendant of the sacred groves of pre-Christian Celtic religion.

Teilo's apple-tree was not the only Celtic sacred tree to find a place in Welsh Christian tradition. The rowan-tree or mountain-ash had always been considered to have protective qualities against evil spirits and this idea persisted until relatively recently. It was given respectability by the belief that Christ's cross had been made from a rowan-tree, which was why its berries looked like drops of his blood.[35] Like Teilo and Samson's conversion of a pre-Christian fertility symbol into a sign of the abundance and goodness of God's creation, this Christianization of the rowan reflects the way in which Celtic Christianity was sometimes able to absorb earlier beliefs and customs, though Dafydd ap Gwilym's poem shows that the process was not always long-lasting or wholly successful.

3. 'Forty days of drops of water...'

hen the fifteenth-century Carmarthenshire poet Lewys Glyn Cothi composed an elegy to Morgan, son of the famous soldier Sir Dafydd Gam, he wrote that

> *Gwlad Vrychan am Vorgan vydd*
> *Ail i gawod ŵyl Gewydd.*
> *Deugain niau davnau dwvr*
> *Ar ruddiau yw'r aweddwvr.* [36]

('Brychan's land will be like a shower on Cewydd's feast-day. Forty days of drops of water on cheeks [i.e. tears] will be the downpour.')

Cewydd was the Welsh equivalent of St Swithin (or Swithun). The belief was widespread throughout south Wales that if it rained on his feast-day it would continue to rain for the next forty days. The Welsh saint became popularly known as *'Hen Gewydd y Glaw'* ('Old Cewydd of the Rain') in Glamorgan, while his festival was called *'Dygwyl Gawau'*. The latter seems to have been transferred at some point from the second of July to the fifteenth (the dates respectively of St Swithin's death and the translation of his remains). [37]

Rain saints are not uncommon in other parts of Europe. Baring Gould and Fisher mention examples from England, France, Belgium, Germany and the Tyrol, while also noting that St Peter is the rain saint in north Wales. They remark of Cewydd that

> No tradition remains to tell us how he became the Welsh S. Swithun. The idea is probably derived from some general pre-Christian belief regarding the meteorologically prophetic character of some day about that period of the year. [38]

Silvan Evans noted that there was a popular belief in Dyfed that the Flood began on the fifteenth of July, the feast of Cewydd and Swithin, and lasted for forty days. The curious calendar in the *Llyfr Plygain* of 1612 however, based partially on a list published by the Puritans in 1578, gives the seventeenth of May as the date on which *'Noah aeth ir Arch ac y dechr. diliw'* ('Noah went into the Ark and the flood began'). [39]

What distinguishes Cewydd from the other rain saints is his name, which is very close to *'cawod'*, the Welsh word for a shower. Silvan Evans was even tempted to suggest that *'Dygwyl Gawau'* might be an abbreviation of *'Dygwyl Gawodau'* ('the feast-day of showers'). [40] The Celtic pantheon included Taranis, the thunder-god, whose name

83

survives in the Welsh word *'taran'* (thunder). The worship of Taranis displayed the darkest side of pre-Christian Celtic religion: 'human sacrifices were offered to him by being burnt alive in tree-trunks.'[41] The link between *'taran'* and Taranis suggests the possibility that Cewydd might have originally been a rain deity, probably with a much more limited cult than that of the thunder-god, whose name influenced, or was influenced by, the words for showers of rain (*'cawodau'* or *'cawodydd'*, which often becomes *'cawedydd'* in dialect).

Such a theory assumes that Cewydd was not an historical figure. Silvan Evans and Baring Gould and Fisher were convinced of the historicity of the saint, believing him to be the son of the Pictish king Caw. Their source for this was the *Iolo MSS.*, which are now regarded as extremely unreliable. There are churches dedicated to the saint, most notably in Radnorshire, but even these may reflect the Christianization of a pagan cult rather than the existence of a sixth-century holy man named Cewydd.[42]

An alternative suggestion is that Cewydd was a genuine figure, perhaps a hermit in the Aberedw area, who acquired a reputation for manipulating the weather. Rain-makers are not unknown in the traditions of the Welsh saints. Samson was credited with posthumously producing a shower to put out a fire in his former monastery after his aid had been invoked. *'Y Saith Gefnder'* ('the Seven Cousins'—a group of saints which included Beuno, Cybi, David, Deiniol, Seiriol and Cawrdaf, Cynfarch or Cadfarch) were said to have gone to Rome to pray for rain after a three year drought, *'ar dafn cyntaf a syrthiodd ar lyvr Cadfarch Sant'* ('and the first drop fell on St Cadfarch's book').[43]

MacCulloch refers to the part played by priests in some rain-making rituals still extant in rural France at the time when he was writing (1911). He describes the custom at Baranton where the priest and people process to the local fountain, where they pray for rain and 'the priest then dips his foot in the water, or throws some of it on the rocks.' He comments that

the presence of the Christian priest points to the fact that, formerly, a Druid was necessary as the rain producer. In some cases the priest has inherited through long ages the rain-making or tempest-quelling powers of the pagan priesthood, and is often besought to exercise them.[44]

Some of the same ideas linger on in the remoter parts of rural Wales. On being inducted to his first living in the depths of the countryside a town-bred Anglican priest can still be startled to discover that some

84

of his older parishioners expect him to have at least a partial competence in controlling the elements—something for which his theological college is unlikely to have prepared him. The tradition of *'Hen Gewydd y Glaw'* and the residual demand for rain-making (or preventing) priests may seem nothing more than curious superstitions rooted in pre-Christian beliefs which somehow lived on in the Celtic Christian world. However they also reflect a very definite view of rainfall as a God-given life-giving force. In a Wales whose hills have been poisoned by radioactive rain from Chernobyl and whose lakes, rivers and trees are suffering from the effects of acid rain the old wisdom which regarded even the rain as essentially sacred contains an important message.

NOTES

[1] John Manley, *Atlas of Prehistoric Britain* (London, 1989), p.108.
[2] Anne Ross, *Everyday Life of the Pagan Celts* (London, 1972), p.193. J.A. MacCulloch, *The Religion of the Ancient Celts* (London, 1991), pp.329-31, also writes of the magical powers ascribed to certain stones in pre-Christian Celtic religion.
[3] Davies, *Wales in the Early Middle Ages*, p.215.
[4] Thomas Taylor, *The Life of St. Samson of Dôl* (London, 1925), pp.4-5.
[5] Taylor, *Life of St. Samson*, pp.49-50.
[6] Taylor, *Life of St. Samson*, p.49.
[7] Arthur G. Langdon, *Old Cornish Crosses* (Exeter, 1988), pp.240-1.
[8] Taylor, *Life of St. Samson*, p.49.
[9] F.E. Halliday, *The Legend of the Rood* (London, 1955), pp.11-18.
[10] Robert Longsworth, *The Cornish Ordinalia: Religion and Dramaturgy* (Cambridge, Massachusetts, 1967), p.2.
[11] Thomas, *Celtic Britain*, p.171.
[12] *Dictionary of Welsh Biography*, pp.902-3; Taylor, *Life of St. Samson*, p.xli.
[13] Henken, *The Welsh Saints*, p.103.
[14] Baring Gould and Fisher, *Lives*, IV, 170; Henken, *Traditions of the Welsh Saints*, p.119; Francis Jones, *The Holy Wells of Wales* (Cardiff, 1954), p.44 (note).
[15] Jones, *Holy Wells*, p.44 (note).
[16] *Dictionnaire des Saints bretons*, p.324.
[17] Green, *Gods of the Celts*, p.21.
[18] Anne Ross, *Pagan Celtic Britain: Studies in Iconography and Tradition* (London, 1967), p.38.
[19] Nennius, *British History*, p.45.
[20] *The Liber Landavensis, Llyfr Teilo*, edited and translated by W.J. Rees (Llandovery, 1840), p.346.

[21] *Dictionnaire des Saints bretons*, p.342.

[22] Jones, *Holy Wells*, p.18.

[23] Rhiannon Ifans, *Sêrs a Rybana: Astudiaeth o'r Canu Gwasael* (Llandysul, 1983), p.83.

[24] Ifans, *Sêrs a Rybana*, p.82.

[25] Ifans, *Sêrs a Rybana*, p.145.

[26] Ifans, *Sêrs a Rybana*, p.87.

[27] Ifans, *Sêrs a Rybana*, p.88.

[28] *Llyfr Du Caerfyrddin*, p.xxxvii.

[29] *Llyfr Du Caerfyrddin*, p.28.

[30] Helen Fulton, *Dafydd ap Gwilym and the European Context* (Cardiff, 1989), pp.164-5.

[31] *Gwaith Dafydd ap Gwilym*, edited by Thomas Parry (Cardiff, 1963), pp.323-4.

[32] *50 o Gywyddau Dafydd ap Gwilym*, edited by Alan Llwyd (Swansea, 1980), pp.55-6.

[33] *50 o Gywyddau*, p.56.

[34] *Geiriadur Prifysgol Cymru*, edited by R.J. Thomas and others (Cardiff, 1950—), I, 266.

[35] Evan Isaac, *Coelion Cymru* (Aberystwyth, 1938), p.159.

[36] *Gwaith Lewis Glyn Cothi*, p.5.

[37] D. Silvan Evans, 'Dygwyl Gewydd', *Y Brython*, edited by D. Silvan Evans (1858-9), reprint edited by Robert Isaac Jones, 'Alltud Eifion' (Tremadog, 1901), p.371; Baring Gould and Fisher, *Lives*, II, 117.

[38] Baring Gould and Fisher, *Lives*, II, 117.

[39] Evans, 'Dygwyl Gewydd', pp.372-3; John Ballinger and John Fisher, *Llyfr Plygain 1612* (Cardiff, 1931), pp.17, 256.

[40] Evans, 'Dygwyl Gewydd', p.371.

[41] Green, *Gods of the Celts*, p.66.

[42] Evans, 'Dygwyl Gewydd', p.371; Baring Gould and Fisher, *Lives*, II, 115-6; Henken, *Traditions of the Welsh Saints*, pp.260-1.

[43] Henken, *The Welsh Saints*, pp.67, 70-1; Henken, *Traditions of the Welsh Saints*, pp.293-4.

[44] Mac Culloch, *Religion of the Ancient Celts*, pp.321-2.61.

Chapter Six:

THE HEALING WATERS

1. 'The water is held to be extremely beneficial...'

In the second half of the eighteenth century the antiquary Thomas Pennant visited the village of Llandegla in Denbighshire. He passed the church, 'dedicated to St. *Tecla*, virgin and martyr; who, after her conversion by St. *Paul*, suffered under *Nero* at *Iconium*,' and a couple of hundred yards later came to a spot called Gwern Degla ('Tegla's Alder-trees') where 'rises a small spring.' This was Ffynnon Degla, one of the most famous sacred springs in Wales. Pennant described the strange and complicated ritual which sometimes took place there:

> The water is under the tutelage of the saint; and to this day is held to be extremely beneficial in the *Clwyf Tegla,* St. *Tecla*'s disease, or the falling-sickness. The patient washes his limbs in the well; makes an offering into it of four pence; walks round it three times; and thrice repeats the Lord's prayer. These ceremonies are never begun till after sun-set, in order to inspire the votaries with greater awe. If the afflicted be of the male-sex, like *Socrates,* he makes an offering of a cock to his *Esculapius* or rather to *Tecla Hygeia*; if of the fair sex, a hen. The fowl is carried in a basket, first round the well; after that into the church-yard; where the same orisons, and the same circum-ambulations are performed round the church. The votary then enters the church; gets under the communion-table; lies down with the Bible under his or her head; is covered with the carpet or cloth, and rests there till break of day; departing after offering six pence, and leaving the fowl in the church. If the bird dies, the cure is supposed to have been effected, and the disease transferred to the devoted victim.[1]

Francis Jones comments on this curious rite: 'It is clear that at Ffynnon Degla we are in the presence of stark paganism.'[2] The local Rural Dean in 1749 seems to have agreed. In that year he 'gave strict charge to the parish clerk at his peril to discourage that superstitious practice, and to admit none into the church at night on that errand.' The Rector of Llandegla who wrote a description of the ceremony for the antiquary Edward Lhuyd in 1699 was apparently more sympathetic towards it. He informed him that a thirteen year old epileptic called John Abraham had been cured of his disease by going through the ritual. The Rural Dean's attempts at suppression seem to have met with little success. The last known attempt to cure someone of '*Clwyf Tegla*' in the traditional manner was as late as 1813. The patient, Evan Edwards, was the sexton of Llandegla's son.[3]

There can be no doubt that the Ffynnon Degla ceremonies had their origin in the pre-Christian period. When Alwyn D. Rees excavated the well he discovered a large number of pieces of quartz and calcite which had apparently been thrown into the *ffynnon* as offerings of some kind. He could not find anyone locally who remembered hearing about this custom, though similar practices are associated with other holy wells elsewhere in the Celtic lands. The white stones must have had a special place in the ritual of the well at some early period. Rees noted that the popular Celtic belief in the magical potency of white quartz and rock crystal 'appears to date back at least to Bronze Age times.'[4] As for the use of cockerels at Ffynnon Degla, Baring Gould and Fisher remarked that the birds had long been associated with epilepsy. They went on to describe an unpleasant 'cure' still current in the north of Scotland at the beginning of this century. It involved burying a black cock alive, along with a lock of an epileptic's hair and some parings of his nails, at the spot where the patient had first fallen.[5] As Pennant mentions above, the Greeks and Romans had sacrificed cockerels to Aesculapius, the god of health and healing, in thanks for recovery from an illness.

However, despite the very obvious pre-Christian elements which they contained, the Ffynnon Degla rites had undergone a conscious and progressive Christianization by the time that Pennant visited the spot. The spring itself had been put under the guardianship of a Christian saint many centuries before. Admittedly Tegla is a rather shadowy figure. The identification with Paul's virgin-martyr friend Thecla is unlikely and may well stem from a typical medieval confusion of a local Welsh saint with a figure better known to Christendom at large.[6] The strongest possibility is that Tegla was a woman hermit who settled near the ancient healing spring, probably in the sixth century. Llandegla Church would eventually have been built on the site of her cell.

Not only had the well been dedicated to Tegla, Christian elements had also been added to the ritual itself. The prayer offered was the Lord's prayer. It was repeated three times both by the well and outside the church, while the patient also walked three times round the well and three times round the church. This implied an invocation of the Trinity, though the pagan Celts had also regarded three as an extremely significant number. Remaining in the church until daybreak was probably a very ancient practice, whereas the use of the communion-table and the Bible in the ritual presumably date from after the Reformation. There had obviously been a deliberate attempt to incorporate important Christian symbols into the original rite.

From the earliest times Ffynnon Degla had apparently offered a ray of hope to parents whose children were epileptic. Suppressing the ceremonies at the well would have done nothing to meet the need that those rituals, however bizarre, attempted to address. The continuation of the rites at Tegla's spring and their development into a somewhat curious mixture of the Christian and the pre-Christian suggests an inclusive rather than an exclusive approach to religion. This seems to have been characteristic of Celtic Christianity in Wales, particularly where it came into contact with customs connected with healing. Looked at sympathetically the eighteenth-century accounts of the Ffynnon Degla ceremonies reveal not 'stark paganism' but rather a fairly crude but not wholly misguided attempt to Christianize a cult that seemed to offer the possibility of some sort of healing for children who could not be helped by the limited medical knowledge of the time. Certainly that was the way in which the Rector of Llandegla who wrote to Edward Lhuyd saw the ancient tradition of his parish. Others, like the hostile Rural Dean fifty years later, saw it in a different light.

In Pembrokeshire there was another sacred well which had a ritual that seems to have been at least as old as that at Ffynnon Degla. The well at Llandeilo Llwydiarth near Maenclochog was visited by Sir John Rhys at the turn of the century. He was told that its water was able to cure whooping-cough. It was only effective however if drawn out of the well by the heir of the Melchior family, who had occupied Llandeilo farm house for several centuries. The patient had to drink the water from 'the upper portion of a thick, strong skull,' which Rhys was told was that of St Teilo himself.

Rhys was later informed how the object was supposed to have got there. It was said that a beautiful maidservant from the Pembrokeshire Llandeilo had nursed the saint when he was on his death-bed. As Teilo lay dying he made her solemnly pledge that exactly a year after his burial at Llandeilo Fawr in Carmarthenshire she would take his skull back to her own Llandeilo 'to leave it there to be a blessing to

89

coming generations of men, who, when ailing, would have their health restored by drinking water out of it.'[7] Baring Gould and Fisher give a detailed description of the skull. They comment that it is clearly that of a young man, and cannot therefore have belonged to Teilo, who is said to have died at an advanced age.[8] Francis Jones, however, says that it may have belonged to a young woman. By 1954 the ancient fragment of bone had disappeared.[9]

Rhys was convinced that the skull had pre-Christian origins and everything that is known about pagan Celtic religion supports the idea.[10] Miranda Green notes how evidence of the grim practices of human sacrifice and head-hunting or head-collecting is supplied by both archaeological and literary sources. Livy tells how a North Italian tribe used the gilded skull of a captured Roman general as a cult-vessel. In Irish tradition the supernaturally large head of the Ulsterman Conall Cernach had magic powers, and it was said that the men of Ulster would gain strength from drinking from it. A skull was found in the well dedicated to the northern Romano-British goddess Coventina at Carrawburgh and another in the Caves Inn well in Warwickshire.[11]

Those who first drank from *'Penglog Teilo'* ('Teilo's skull') centuries before the saint was born presumably hoped to acquire some special quality associated with the person to whom it had belonged. This may have been linked from the very beginning with an additional belief in the healing virtues of the well. Later, when the cult had been absorbed into Christianity and linked with the saint who had founded the little church nearby, the skull was seen as the vehicle of Teilo's miraculous healing powers.

There is a strange and fascinating footnote to the history of the well-cult at Llandeilo Llwydiarth which may help to explain the true significance of such apparently ambiguous places of devotion. During the First World War rural west Wales began to feel the devastating effects of a brutal conflict that tore young men away from their homes and sent them across the sea to die in the hell of the Flanders trenches. There was an overwhelming desire for peace. Quite unexpectedly people started visiting Ffynnon Deilo at Llandeilo Llwydiarth and drinking from the holy skull, not because they were looking for a cure for whooping-cough, but because they believed that by doing so they would somehow help to bring an end to the slaughter.[12]

This instinctive turning to an ancient ritual for consolation and hope at a time of desolation parallels the actions of the parents of the young epileptics who went to Ffynnon Degla. It may have been

90

unorthodox, but at the heart of the Celtic Christian tradition there seems to be a quiet suspicion that God's actions are not necessarily limited by officially accepted definitions of orthodoxy.

2. 'Musk and balm in the midst of the world...'

ater is essential for human existence. It is therefore not surprising that *'ffynhonnau'* (springs or wells) played a central part in the development of society in Wales from the very beginning. Their fundamental importance meant that they quickly acquired a religious significance. Anne Ross describes springs, wells and rivers as 'a focal point of Celtic cult practice and ritual.'[13] The sacred and the practical were combined. Many holy wells or springs remained a major source of drinking water for remote rural communities until relatively recently.[14]

Certain springs also became known for their healing qualities. Their reputations often persist. When I first became vicar of the Carmarthenshire hill parish of Llanfihangel Rhos-y-corn one of my churchwardens advised me that if ever I had trouble with my eyes I should bathe them in water from Pistyll Jac, a local spring. Ffynnon Degla and Ffynnon Deilo are thus not isolated phenomena, although the particular rituals associated with them have few parallels. Francis Jones' admittedly incomplete survey recorded 935 healing springs and wells in Wales, 437 of which were associated with Christian saints.[15] Of these the one which during the later Middle Ages became the most famous of all was the well of Gwenfrewi (sometimes called Gwenffrewi) or Winifred at Holywell (Treffynnon) in Flintshire.

The problems connected with the legend of Gwenfrewi have been hinted at in chapter two. The earliest life of the saint dates from the eleventh or possibly the twelfth century and several others followed.[16] She was said to have lived in the first half of the seventh century and to have been Beuno's niece. A young nobleman named Caradog made advances to her, which she rejected, running off to her uncle's chapel. Before she reached it Caradog caught up with her, swiping off her head with his sword. The rock opened at the spot where her head landed and a spring began to gush forth. Beuno emerged from his chapel and cursed Caradog so forcefully that the young man melted away like wax. Then the saint successfully managed to restore Gwenfrewi's head and she made a complete recovery, though she still had a scar on her neck. The spring continued to flow.

After her restoration to life Gwenfrewi was supposed to have founded some sort of convent at Holywell, initially under her uncle's guidance. She later became the superior of an already established community of holy virgins at Gwytherin. During this phase of her life Gwenfrewi's name is linked with those of the hermits Deifer, Sadwrn and Eleri, to whom she turned for advice. She died at Gwytherin fifteen years after the miracle at Holywell. In 1138 her relics were moved to Shrewsbury Abbey with a great deal of ceremony.[17] The status of her new resting place was one of the reasons why she began to attract the attention of medieval hagiographers.

Baring Gould and Fisher are convinced that Gwenfrewi existed. They write that

On the whole, we are not justified in rejecting the broad outline of the story of S. Winefred because of the fabulous and adventitious matter that has grown about it, and we are disposed to regard her relations with Deifer, Sadwrn and Eleri, and her residence at Gwytherin as the most certain points in her story. That as a young girl she was solicited by a certain cub of a noble, that she resisted him, and that she was scratched in the scuffle with him is all that can be admitted; out of that a huge overgrowth of fable has arisen.[18]

The historical Gwenfrewi was thus almost certainly an early seventh century woman ascetic.[19] She may well have lived at Holywell before she moved to Gwytherin, which is how her name came to be connected with an already existing water cult.

The legend of Gwenfrewi's decapitation and restoration includes some motifs which appear elsewhere. Several Celtic women saints are said to have had their heads cut off, and in some cases springs also appeared where the heads touched the ground.[20] This suggests memories of a connection between pagan Celtic head cults and water cults. It may even imply a practice of sacrificing a young woman at a holy well—which may explain why the supposed skull of Teilo at the Pembrokeshire Ffynnon Deilo was probably that of a young woman. It is also significant that Gwenfrewi's head was not the only one which Beuno was supposed to have restored.[21] This again may be an echo of some kind of pagan ritual, since, as was noted in chapter four, the cult of Beuno seems to have absorbed several elements from pre-Christian Celtic religion.

The spring at Holywell and its surroundings possessed certain key physical features which left their mark on the development of the story. The well contained red-veined stones on which grew a sweet-smelling crimson moss. Ffynnon Wenfrewi is described as 'the most copious natural spring in Britain' and although it is intensely cold it apparently never freezes. [22] It is hardly surprising that such a remarkable phenomenon should have acquired a religious significance. The spring had presumably had a reputation for its healing qualities long before the seventh century. The stones and the moss became seen as reminders of Gwenfrewi's temporary martyrdom.

However both the water and the 'blood' soon attained an extra significance. They became linked with two of the most powerful Christian symbols: the water of baptism and the blood of Christ. As a result they were thought to possess a sacramental quality, as is shown in a beautiful *cywydd* to Gwenfrewi written by Tudur Aled (c.1465-c.1525), one of the greatest Welsh poets:

> *Main gwyarog mewn gweryd,*
> *Mwsg a bawm ym mysg y byd;*
> *Man pêr ar bob maen purwyn,*
> *Main ag ôl gwaed mwnwgl gwyn;*
> *Beth ydyw'r ôl byth a drig?*
> *Band i gwaed bendigedig?*
> *Dagrau fel cawod egroes,*
> *Defni Crist, o fannau croes;*
> *Daioni corff dyn, o caid, —*
> *Derbyn deigr dŵr bendigaid;*
> *Dyfriw gwaed, fal dwfr a gwin,*
> *Dwyn iwch wyrthiau dan chwerthin;*
> *Crechwen gwraidd crychwyn groywddwfr,*
> *Coel iechyd ynt—clochau dwfr;*
> *Aber brwd o'r berw briwdan,*
> *Os brwd gwlith yr Ysbryd Glân;*
> *Irder byd yw'r dŵr bedydd,*
> *A elwir ffons olew'r ffydd.* [23]

('Red-spotted stones in earth, musk and balm in the midst of the world; a sweet spot on every pure white stone, stones with a trace of blood from a white/holy neck. What is the mark that lasts forever? The band of her blessed blood. Tears like a shower of rose-hips, drops of Christ from the marks of the cross. It would do good to a man's body to receive tears of holy water. Droplets of blood, like water and wine, laughingly bringing you miracles. The shouts of laughter from the source of the rippling fresh water are an omen of health—bells of the water. An ardent stream from the fire-flashing foam, the thrilling unction of the Holy Spirit; the water of baptism is the sap of the world, which is called the fount of the oil of faith.')

Tudur Aled's lines forcefully convey the impact on the religious imagination of this water bubbling forth from ground speckled with red-stained stones covered with scented moss. The truth or fiction of the legend about the saint was not important. What mattered was that her spring had become a visible, tangible and indeed audible expression of God's presence as a life-giving, healing force in the midst of a world afflicted by pain and disease.

Gwenfrewi's spring was not the only the one to be associated with the waters of baptism. Francis Jones describes 'the use of water drawn from holy wells for baptism' as 'an ancient custom.' He says that hymns were sometimes sung while the water was being carried from the spring to the font. This practice survived into the eighteenth century. The literary cleric and antiquary Gwallter Mechain (Walter Davies, 1761-1849) was baptized with water from Ffynnon Armon in Montgomeryshire.[24] Thomas Pennant refers to such baptisms as among 'customs that have gradually been dropped':

If there be a *Ffynnon Fair,* the well of our Lady, or of any other saint, the water for baptism was always brought from thence, and after the ceremony was over, old women were very fond of washing their eyes in the water of the font.[25]

It is hardly surprising that water which had always been regarded as having a sacred quality should have been felt to be particularly appropriate for a Christian sacrament. The Celtic saints in Wales normally chose to establish their cells and churches near both a river and a spring. The result is that, as Siân Victory has observed, 'Almost every church in Wales today can boast its holy well near by, though patient hunting through the long grass may be needed to locate it.'[26] It seems certain that the Christian holy men and women who settled by these sacred springs in the sixth and seventh centuries took water from them to baptize their first converts, symbolically Christianizing the wells in the process.

3. 'Dwynwen will not hinder adultery...'

ome holy wells developed secondary functions which illustrate how easily the practices connected with them could degenerate into a form of folk magic. One such ambiguous spring was Ffynnon Ddwynwen in Anglesey. Dwynwen or Dwyn is listed as one of the twenty-five daughters of Brychan, the fifth-century king of Brycheiniog. She is described in the *Myvyrian Archaiology* as the Welsh equivalent of Venus.[27] It is not certain how she acquired this reputation. Baring Gould and Fisher reprint a colourful legend about Dwynwen and Maelon Dafodrill, her unfortunate lover, in which Dwynwen is cured of her infatuation while Maelon gets frozen into a lump of ice. God then grants the maiden three requests.

She first desired that Maelon should be unfrozen; next that her supplications should always be granted in favour of all true-hearted lovers, so that they should either obtain the objects of their affection, or be cured of their love-passion; and, thirdly, that henceforth she should never wish to be married: and the three requests were conceded to her, whereupon she took the veil, and became a Saint. Every faithful lover who subsequently invoked her was either relieved from his passion, or obtained the object of his affection.[28]

The source of this story is the literary forger Iolo Morganwg and there can be little doubt that it is almost entirely the product of his over-fertile imagination.

Nevertheless Dwynwen's reputation as the patron saint of Welsh lovers goes back well into the Middle Ages. Dafydd ap Gwilym addressed a *cywydd* to her statue, asking it to take a message of love to Morfudd.[29] In the poem he refers to the saint's capacity for healing both physical ills and the mental torment of frustrated lovers:

> *Dwynwen deigr arien degwch,*
> *Da y gûyr o gôr fflamgwyr fflwch*
> *Dy ddelw aur diddoluriaw*
> *Digion druain ddynion draw.*
> *Dyn a wylio, gloywdro glân,*
> *Yn dy gôr, Indeg eirian,*
> *Nid oes glefyd na bryd brwyn*
> *A êl ynddo o Landdwyn.*[30]

('Dwynwen, fair as tears of hoar-frost, from your chancel lit with the flames of large wax candles your golden image well knows how

95

to alleviate the pain and anguish of wretched men. The man who keeps vigil (a time of shining holiness) in your choir, radiant Indeg, will not take sickness or sadness of mind away with him from Llanddwyn.')

Dafydd's poems also underlines Dwynwen's questionable moral position. Although she herself was supposed to be a chaste virgin she had become the saint to whom would-be adulterers like Dafydd turned for help:

> *Cymysg lateirwydd flwyddyn,*
> *Â rhadau Duw rhod a dyn.*
> *Nid rhaid, ddelw euraid ddilyth,*
> *Yt ofn pechawd, fethlgnawd fyth.*
> *Nid adwna, da ei dangnef,*
> *Duw a wnaeth; nid ei o nef.*
> *Ni'th ŵyl mursen eleni*
> *Yn hustyng yn yng â ni.*
> *Ni rydd Eiddig ddig ddygnbwyll*
> *War ffon i ti, wyry ei phwyll.*[31]

('Mix being a love-messenger for a year with bringing God's blessings to man. Unfailing golden image, you need not be afraid of sin, the flesh's constant snare. God, whose peace is good, will not undo what he has done, you will not be thrown out of heaven. No prudish girl will see you whispering to us in a corner. Angry, cruel-minded Eiddig [Morfudd's jealous husband] will not hit you with his stick, chaste-minded one.')

A slightly later poet, Dafydd Llwyd of Mathafarn (c.1395-c.1486), also sees comic potential in Dwynwen's paradoxical status. In a satirical attack on jealous women he describes the saint as *'diwair iawn'* ('very chaste') but says that *'Dwynwen ni ludd odineb'* ('Dwynwen will not hinder adultery').[32]

Ffynnon Ddwynwen's reputation may have its origins in a pre-Christian fertility rite. Miranda Green has noted how the concepts of healing and regeneration (linked with fertility) seem to coincide in many pagan Celtic water cults, paricularly those associated with goddesses.[33] Dwynwen's well also fulfilled this dual function. Richard Fenton described a visit to Llanddwyn at the beginning of the last century:

> The spring is now choak'd up by the sands, at which an old woman officiated, and prognosticated the lover's success from the motions

96

of some eels who issued out of the sides of the well on spreading the suitor's handkerchief on the surface. The saint was also petitioned for the cure of divers diseases, particularly aches [? rheumatism].[34]

By 1862 the well had long disappeared, but apparently the young women of the neighbourhood still used 'the water nearest to it' in the hope that Dwynwen would bless their love lives.[35] The water referred to must be that of Crochan Llanddwyn ('Llanddwyn's Cauldron'), described by Baring Gould and Fisher as 'a small wishing-well . . . still frequented by love-sick lads and lasses.'[36]

The editor of *Cymru Fu* remarked that it was a pity that Ffynnon Ddwynwen was not flowing once more, and that Ffynnon Elian had not been buried by the sand instead.[37] He was referring to the 'cursing well' at Llanelian in Denbighshire. This had originally been visited by those who wanted to heal their sick children. They would empty the well three times, and give a groat or the equivalent in bread to the keeper of the well—a practice which Francis Jones describes as 'a known pagan ritual' with a long history.[38] At some point in the eighteenth century the function of the well began to change until it became 'the most dreadful of all the Welsh Holy Wells.'[39]

Thomas Pennant's account gives the impression that Ffynnon Elian may have begun as a healing well and then been 'made the instrument of discovering thieves, and of recovering stolen goods' until it finally developed into a place where people went 'to imprecate their neighbors, and to request the saint to afflict with sudden death, or with some great misfortune, any persons who may have offended them.' Pennant himself had been threatened with such a curse by 'a fellow (who imagined I had injured him).'[40] Like Ffynnon Ddwynwen the well had its guardians, who made a great deal of money from performing the cursing ceremony when Ffynnon Elian was at the height of its notoriety. The most famous of these were the 'priestess' Mrs Hughes and her successor John Evans, a tailor, better known as 'Jac Ffynnon Elian'. They would also remove curses for an appropriate fee. In January 1829 the well was filled in. A few years earlier Jac Ffynnon Elian had been imprisoned in an attempt to put an end to his activities.[41]

There was a local tradition that Ffynnon Elian appeared when a passing hermit, having suddenly been taken ill, sat down by the roadside and prayed for a drink of water. The spring gushed forth and having drunk from it he recovered. In thanks he prayed that the spring might be the means by which all who asked in faith might be

97

granted their wishes.[42] It appears that he was unaware of the dark element in human nature which surfaced among the well's devotees in the eighteenth century, if not before. Francis Jones refers to several other cursing wells in Wales. He is not able to establish their antiquity, but notes the discovery of a lead *defixio* (curse-tablet) from a Roman reservoir in Bath.[43] This would seem to suggest that some of the rituals of commination at these wells may have had their origins in the pre-Christian period.

Ffynnon Ddwynwen and Ffynnon Elian, for all their fame in Welsh folklore, are essentially aberrations. With both wells healing became a secondary function which eventually vanished altogether. Almost all the other springs associated with saints preserved their therapeutic reputation. This had been carried over from the pre-Christian period. Miranda Green writes of 'the florescence of a great Celtic cult of healing—the main role of sacred water before and during the Romano-Celtic period in Gaul and Britain.'[44] The holy wells were absorbed into Christianity by the use of their water for baptism, but their healing powers were still respected and cherished. The Christian Celts in Wales continued to regard pure, clear, flowing water as a sacred source and symbol of life and wholeness—in Tudur Aled's words *'coel iechyd'* and *'irder byd'*—an 'omen of health' and the 'sap of the world'.

NOTES

[1] Thomas Pennant, *Tours in Wales,* edited by John Rhys (Caernarfon, 1883), II, 15-16.
[2] Jones, *Holy Wells,* p.104.
[3] Baring Gould and Fisher, *Lives,* IV, 220-1.
[4] Alwyn D. Rees, 'Notes on the significance of white stones in Celtic archaeology and folklore with reference to recent excavations at Ffynnon Degla, Denbighshire,' *Bulletin of the Board of Celtic Studies,* XIII, Pt.1 (1935), pp.87-90.
[5] Baring Gould and Fisher, *Lives,* IV, 221-2.
[6] Baring Gould and Fisher, *Lives,* IV, 219.
[7] John Rhys, *Celtic Folklore: Welsh and Manx* (London, 1980), I, 397-9.
[8] Baring Gould and Fisher, *Lives,* IV, 239-40.
[9] Jones, *Holy Wells,* p.116, note.
[10] Rhys, *Celtic Folklore,* I, 400.
[11] Green, *Gods of the Celts,* pp.28-32, 157, 166.
[12] Jones, *Holy Wells,* p.81.
[13] Ross, *Pagan Celtic Britain,* p.20.
[14] This was the case with Ffynnon Deilo in my own village of Brechfa.
[15] Jones, *Holy Wells,* p.97.
[16] Baring Gould and Fisher, *Lives,* III, 185-7.
[17] Baring Gould and Fisher, *Lives,* III, 190.

[18] Baring Gould and Fisher, *Lives,* III, 192-3.

[19] This view is also accepted by Professor Thomas Pierce Jones in his article in the *Dictionary of Welsh Biography,* pp.324-5.

[20] Baring Gould and Fisher, *Lives,* III, 191.

[21] Henken, *Traditions of the Welsh Saints,* pp.77-9.

[22] Baring Gould and Fisher, *Lives,* III, 191-2, 194-5.

[23] *Gwaith Tudur Aled,* edited by T. Gwynn Jones (Cardiff. 1926), II, 524-5.

[24] Jones, *Holy Wells,* p.81.

[25] Pennant, *Tours in Wales,* III, 150.

[26] Victory, *Celtic Church in Wales,* p.25.

[27] *The Myvyrian Archaiology of Wales: Collected out of Ancient Manuscripts,* edited by Owen Jones, Edward Williams and William Owen Pughe (Denbigh, 1870), p.423, note.

[28] Baring Gould and Fisher, *Lives,* II, 388.

[29] Rachel Bromwich, *Dafydd ap Gwilym: A Selection of Poems* (Llandysul, 1982), p.126, suggests that Iolo Morganwg's legend of Dwynwen was based on his conjectural interpretation of some lines from this poem.

[30] *Gwaith Dafydd ap Gwilym,* p.256.

[31] *Gwaith Dafydd ap Gwilym,* p.256.

[32] *Gwaith Dafydd Llwyd o Fathafarn,* edited by W. Leslie Richards (Cardiff, 1964), p.174.

[33] Green, *Gods of the Celts,* p.165.

[34] *Archaeologia Cambrensis* (6th series), XV (1898), p.371.

[35] *Cymru Fu* (Wrexham, 1862), pp.423-4.

[36] Baring Gould and Fisher, *Lives,* II, 391.

[37] *Cymru Fu,* p.424.

[38] Jones, *Holy Wells,* p.103.

[39] Baring Gould and Fisher, *Lives,* II, 440.

[40] Pennant, *Tours in Wales,* III, 149-50.

[41] Baring Gould and Fisher, *Lives,* II, 441-2; Jones, Holy Wells, pp.118-20.

[42] Baring Gould and Fisher, *Lives,* III, 440. They do not record the source of this story.

[43] Jones, *Holy Wells,* pp.117-9; Green, *Gods of the Celts,* pp.24-5.

[44] Green, *Gods of the Celts,* p.150.

PART THREE: LEARNING TO LOVE

Chapter Seven:

HOLY MOTHERS

1. 'Elen Luyddog, who went from Britain to Jerusalem...'

 el achau' (tracing family-trees) has been a Welsh enthusiasm for many centuries. An early example is a collection of genealogies that has survived in one of the Harleian manuscripts. It was probably compiled in Dyfed around the year 954 by a supporter of king Hywel Dda.[1] It includes a list in which it is claimed that the royal family of Dyfed can trace itself back to 'Constans, son of Constantius and Helen luicdauc, who went from Britain to Jerusalem to seek the cross of Christ.'[2] 'Helen luicdauc' is a primitive and slightly corrupt rendering of Elen Luyddog or 'Helen of the Hosts'. 'Constans' is none other than Constantine the Great, the first Christian emperor of Rome.

The twelfth century English writer Henry of Huntingdon recorded an East Anglian tradition that Helena, Constantine's mother, had been the daughter of a British king called Coel (the original 'Old King Cole').[3] Geoffrey of Monmouth repeated the story, writing that

After Coel's death Constantius himself seized the royal crown and married Coel's daughter. Her name was Helen and her beauty was greater than that of any other young woman in the kingdom. For that matter, no more lovely girl could be discovered anywhere. Her father had no other child to inherit the throne, and he had therefore done all in his power which would enable her to rule the country more efficiently after his death. After her marriage with Constantius she had by him a son named Constantine.[4]

Geoffrey's endorsement of the idea that Constantine's mother had been a British princess reinforced the belief in Welsh minds. An early thirteenth-century vernacular history, based broadly on Geoffrey's work, identifies the princess as 'Elen Luydavc'.[5] One modern commentator has noted that Geoffrey completely ignored Helena's 'sainthood and above all...the most celebrated thing in her history, her discovery of the True Cross in Jerusalem.'[6] A medieval Welsh genealogist made up for this by recording that 'Constantine's mother was Elen Luyddog, who won the cross in Jerusalem, and brought part of it to Constantinople, and sent another part to the Britons. . .'[7]

As late as 1740 the Welsh historian Theophilus Evans was still convinced that Elen, the British princess, had given birth to Constantine the Great.[8] But in the nineteenth century less romantic writers began to do their sums. In 1836 Rice Rees, the brilliant young professor of Welsh at Lampeter, calmly demolished the old story:

> Now Constantius visited Britain, for the first time, in 296; and allowing that Constantine was born that year, he could only have been ten years old at the time of his accession to the empire; he was, therefore, not born in Britain. Besides, Helen was the wife of Constantius's younger years, and, as she was divorced by him as early as A.D. 286, ten years before his arrival in this country, she was not likely to have been a Briton.[9]

Helena, Constantine's mother, was in fact a native of Drepanum in Bithynia. Her father is said to have kept an inn there. In January 328, after his mother's death, the emperor renamed the city Helenopolis in her honour.[10]

The belief in a native Elen/Helen somehow connected with the Roman occupation has, however, left its mark on the Welsh landscape. The Roman road between Segontium (Caernarfon) and Maridunum (Carmarthen) is still known as 'Sarn Helen' ('Helen's Causeway'), as is the road which branches off from it towards Llandovery and the gold mines of Dolau Cothi.[11] A twelfth century story explains how they got their name. It tells of how the Roman emperor, Macsen Wledig, had a dream of a beautiful woman with whom he fell hopelessly in love. He sent messengers to look for her and after much searching they found her in a fortress called Caer Aber Seint (Segontium). Macsen married the woman, whose name was Elen Luyddog.

> Thereafter Elen thought to make high roads from one stronghold to another across the Island of Britain. And the roads were made. And for that reason they are called the Roads of Elen of the Hosts, because she was sprung from the Island of Britain, and the men of the Island of Britain would not have made those great hostings for any but her.[12]

Sir Ifor Williams regards this passage as being one of the oldest elements in the story.[13]

104

Macsen Wledig is an historical character. He is otherwise known as Magnus Maximus, a Roman general whose troops proclaimed him emperor in Britain in 383. Some modern Welsh historians regard him as 'the father of the Welsh nation.'[14] In his campaign to overthrow the western emperor Gratian, Macsen denuded Britain of its Roman troops (including the garrison of Segontium), taking them over to Gaul with him. The impact of this momentous event is reflected in the *Trioedd*, which mention that one of the 'Three Levies that departed from this Island, and not one of them came back' went with Elen Luyddog.[15] However several of the old Welsh genealogies make Macsen a descendant of Constantius and the earlier Elen Luyddog. Others name Macsen's wife as 'Elen daughter of Eudaf' (her father in the story).[16] According to Sulpitius Severus she was a devout Christian who on her arrival in Gaul became a devoted admirer of Martin of Tours, preparing the venerable ascetic's food for him and waiting on him in person.[17] It has been suggested that after Macsen's death in 388 Elen returned to Wales where she was regarded as a saint. She and her family are then supposed to have became the focus of a cult among Gallo-Roman exiles and Romano-British refugees in north-west and south-east Wales.[18]

As Rachel Bromwich has pointed out, Geoffrey of Monmouth does not name Macsen's bride, nor does he make any attempt to identify her with Elen Luyddog.[19] There is another tradition which claims that the emperor's wife was the daughter of the king of Erging, whose territory was based on Ariconium (Weston-under-Penyard, a few miles from Ross-on-Wye). Dyfrig (Dubricius) established a monastery at 'Hennllann' (Hentland) near Ariconium in the fifth century. If the area was the home of Macsen's wife, and if she did indeed return there after his death, bringing with her ideas derived from the radical asceticism of Martin of Tours, this may explain why this small Romano-British kingdom came to play a major rôle in the development of early Welsh Christianity.[20]

The original Elen Luyddog was neither Constantine's saintly mother nor Macsen's pious wife. Sir John Rhys was the first to suggest that her origins lay in pre-Christian Celtic religion:

The name Elen still belongs to mythology in Wales: thus in Arvon, for instance, Arianrhod...is said to have had three sisters who lived with her in her castle in the sea. They were named *Gwen* or *Gwennan, Maelan* and *Elen*; all appear, like Arianrhod, to have belonged to the class of goddesses associated with the dawn.[21]

Ifor Williams agreed that Elen was 'one of the goddesses,' though he thought that she might have been a goddess of war because of the way in which her name was connected with the roads along which the Roman soldiers travelled.[22] The location of her cult in Arfon is a reason why she should have become associated with Caer Seint (Segontium).

The process by which a Celtic goddess became identified with a Roman emperor's saintly mother is an intriguing one. Nennius, writing around 800, claimed that Constantine the Great's son had been buried at Caer Seint: 'He sowed three seeds, of gold, of silver, and of bronze, on the pavement of that city, that no man should ever live there poor...'[23] A.S. Loomis comments that the story of Constantine's seeds 'was no doubt devised by antiquaries to explain the large number of coins inscribed with the name.' He notes that 'at least 117 coins of the two Constantines have been dug up at or near Segontium in modern times,' as have 12 coins of Helena, Constantine the Great's mother. He speculates that similar coins inscribed with Helena's name might have led patriotic Welshmen to connect her with Elen Luyddog.[24] Another possibility is mentioned by Rachel Bromwich. She draws attention to Constantine the Great's scheme to repair British roads, remarking that it 'may have assisted the conflation of Elen with St. Helena.'[25]

These may indeed have been factors, but they were probably not the most important ones. Helena was, after the Virgin Mary, the most significant mother in the history of Christendom. Her son was, in Theophilus Evans' words '*y Gwr enwoccaf o'r Byd Chrisnogol*' ('the most famous Man of the Christian World').[26] It was hardly surprising, given the Celtic interest in mother-goddesses, that she should have become linked with a pre-Christian goddess with a similar name. The Christianization of Elen Luyddog and the Celticization of Helena of Drepanum both stem from an underlying concern with sacred motherhood.

An additional element was Helena's visit to the Holy Land, in which the genealogists seem especially interested. Christian pilgrims from Britain had visited Palestine from a very early date. Jerome, writing half a century after Helena's death, recorded how 'The Briton, "sundered from our world," no sooner makes progress in religion than he leaves the setting sun in quest of a spot of which he knows only through Scripture and common report.'[27] It was later claimed that Teilo, David and Padarn had journeyed from Wales to Jerusalem.[28] It is clear that the characteristic Welsh concern with special places included an interest in the religious sites of the Holy Land, which had its origin at the very beginning of Welsh Christianity.

Helena had gone to the Holy Land in 326/7 in order to distract public attention from some domestic difficulties. Constantine's wife had just been compelled to commit suicide after engineering the execution of her stepson. The dowager empress, who was aged almost eighty, intended to restore the family reputation for piety.[29] Her success was spectacular. Constantine had already begun work on the Church of the Holy Sepulchre in Jerusalem. Helena founded churches at Bethlehem and the Mount of Olives, completing a Triad which commemorated the birth, death and resurrection and ascension of Christ.[30] A story later developed that she had found the True Cross on which Jesus had been crucified. This tradition has always been surrounded by controversy, and there is increasing scholarly agreement that the supposed wood of Christ's cross was most probably discovered by Macarius, bishop of Jerusalem, shortly before Helena's visit.[31]

Such nice distinctions had scant meaning for the Welsh Christians who compiled the genealogies. For them Helena had become Elen Luyddog, the saintly Welsh mother of a Christian emperor, who had gone all the way from Britain to the places where Christ was born, suffered, died, rose again and ascended into heaven. There she had uncovered the True Cross and sent part of it back to the Britons, as a sign of God's love for them. Thus the Welsh genius for transmuting, fusing and confusing historical and mythological characters began to bring the Holy Land a little nearer home.

2.   'Brigit, Nurse of Christ . . .'

len Luyddog was not the only Celtic goddess to be transformed into a Christian holy woman. An even more striking example was a saint whose cult flourished throughout the Celtic lands from the Western Isles to the coasts of Brittany. Ffraid, Bride, Brighde, Brighid, Brigit, Brec'hed . . . the name has many forms, but the figure behind them is the same. Ffraid (to keep to the most common Welsh usage) was cloaked with Christian respectability by being identified with an abbess from Kildare, who was said to have lived in the late fifth and early sixth century.[32] Yet, as Proinsias Mac Cana has pointed out, no clear distinction can be made between the goddess and the saint and... in all probability Brighid's great monastery of Kildare was formerly a pagan sanctuary. It is indeed significant that, while Brighid was not a missionary saint nor widely travelled, yet in Ireland she was second only to Patrick in popular favour and dedications to her are found throughout the territories of the insular Celts, so that one can scarcely avoid the conclusion that her widespread cult substantially continues that of her pagan predecessor. [33]

Irish tradition triplicates this pre-Christian Goddess. We are told of three sister goddesses, each called Brighid. The first was an expert in poetry, traditional learning, divination and prophecy, the second was concerned with healing and the third with the craft of the smith. [34] Miranda Green has noted the tendency among the Celts to worship the mother-goddess in a triadic form. Cults of the triple mothers were essentially territorial. [35] Brighid/Ffraid thus emerges as a mother-goddess especially associated with the Goidelic Celts. It has been suggested that there is a connection between churches dedicated to Ffraid in Wales and Irish colonization in the fifth and sixth centuries. [36] However her worship was not confined to the Gaels in the pre-Christian period. She was also Briganti, "The Exalted One", goddess of the Brigantes, the most powerful tribal confederacy in Britain. It seems probable that she was the deity of the Brigantii near Lake Constance as well. [37]

The pre-Christian Brighid/Ffraid was linked with the spring fertility festival of Imbolc or Oímelg. This was held on the first of February at the beginning of the lambing season. Graham Webster remarks that 'Little is known about it, presumably as it was mainly practised by the women and carried out in secret, away from profane male eyes.' [38] Some idea of its rituals can, however, be gathered from the account of Bride's Eve customs in the Western Isles and Ireland given by Alexander Carmichael at the turn of the century. [39] In the Outer Hebrides

> the girls of the townland fashion a sheaf of corn into the likeness of a woman. They dress and deck the figure with shining shells, sparkling crystals, primroses, snowdrops, and any greenery they may obtain ... A specially bright shell or crystal is placed over the heart of the figure ... The girls call the figure 'Bride,' 'Brideag,' Bride, Little Bride, and carry it in procession, singing the song of 'Bride bhoidheach oig nam mile beus,' Beauteous Bride, virgin of a thousand charms. The 'banal Bride,' Bride maiden band, are

clad in white, and have their hair down, symbolising purity and youth. They visit every house, and every person is expected to give a gift to Bride and to make obeisance to her ... Having made the round of the place the girls go to a house to make the 'feis Bride,' Bride feast. They bar the door and secure the windows of the house, and set Bride where she may see and be seen of all.[40]

The pagan festival became the feast-day of the Christian saint. It also brought Ffraid into close proximity with Mary, mother of Christ, whose Purification—'Candlemas' in England and *'Gŵyl Fair y Canhwyllau'* ('The Feast of Mary of the Candles') in Wales—is celebrated on the second of February, forty days after Christmas. The poet Iorwerth Fynglwyd (fl. 1485-1527) wrote a *cywydd* to Ffraid in which he claimed that Jesus himself was responsible for the combination of the festivals which, he added, made Ffraid's feast more important than a Sunday.[41] According to an Irish tradition Brigit/Ffraid once rescued the Mother of God from a crowd by performing a miracle, and was then asked what reward she would like. '"Put my day before your own day" said Brigit.' So Mary did.[42]

In the Celtic mind Mary and Ffraid became closely associated. The ancient mother-goddess was transformed into the 'Mary of the Gael.' The Hebridean islanders called her *'Brighde Moime Chrìosd'*—'Brigid, Nurse of Christ.'[43] They told stories which explained how she came to acquire this name. In one of them Bride/Ffraid was the serving-maid at the inn in Bethlehem. There was a drought and the innkeeper went off to find water, leaving the girl with instructions not to give food, drink or shelter to anyone. Then two strangers arrived at the inn: an old man and a beautiful young woman. They asked for something to eat, water to drink and somewhere to stay. Bride shared her own meagre supply of bread and water with them, but could not give them lodging. After they had thanked her and gone on their way she was astonished to discover that her bannock of bread was still whole and her stoup of water was still full. She went out to see what had happened to the travellers and found that a brilliant golden light was shining over the stable door. Going into the stable she 'was in time to aid and minister to the Virgin Mother and to receive the Child into her arms, for the strangers were Joseph and Mary and the child was Jesus Christ, the Son of God, come to earth and born in the stable of Bethlehem.'[44]

This story influenced the Bride's Eve ceremonies. The especially bright shell or crystal which the girls put over the heart of their model of the saint was called *'reul-iuil Bride'* ('Bride's guiding-star'), because it represented the light over the stable door, which had led her to the Christ-child.[45] Her rôle as the midwife who had delivered Jesus strengthened and sanctified her relationship with the women of the Western Isles. She became *'Brighde bean chomainn'* ('Brigit, woman-comrade'), 'the aid-woman of the mothers of Uist in their humble homes.'[46] In Brittany Brec'hed/Ffraid has a similar function as *'le grand guérisseur des maladies du sexe féminin.'* Her help is sought by childless women who wish to become pregnant, expectant mothers during their pregnancy, nursing mothers who are having trouble with their milk and women suffering from breast cancer.[47]

By transmuting Ffraid, the pre-Christian mother-goddess, into one of its most important saints Celtic Christianity retained a special place for women in its spirituality. Though the cult of Mary became extremely important in the Celtic lands, Christ's mother often tended to be seen in terms which distanced her from many women's lives. Ffraid, however, was able to come closer to her down-to-earth female Celtic devotees, sharing their everyday problems and anxieties. As a woman of South Uist put it:

> I am under the keeping
> Of my Saint Mary;
> My companion beloved
> Is Brigit.[48]

Recording Irish folk belief about her, Lady Gregory wrote that 'there are some say Brigit fostered the Holy Child, and kept an account of every drop of blood he lost through his lifetime. . .'[49] Through this mother-goddess turned midwife and nurse the Celts were able to incorporate the Christ child into their own family and society. A ninth-century Irish monastic poet imagined the famous sixth-century hermit Íte cradling *'Ísucán'* (little Jesus) in her arms:

> It is little Jesus who is nursed by me in my little hermitage. Though a cleric have great wealth, it is all deceitful save Jesukin.[50]

Barriers of time, space and continuity have rarely presented problems for the Celtic imagination. Through Ffraid, with her curious mixture of the supernatural and the homely, that imagination was able to integrate Christ's Incarnation into the daily life of the Celtic lands.

3. 'A maiden called Nonita, exceedingly beautiful . . .'

In his *cywydd* to Ffraid, Iorwerth Fynglwyd described her as *'chwaer i Non'* ('Non's sister').[51] He was apparently referring to the reputation which both saints had acquired for being able to miraculously produce large quantities of drink: Ffraid's beer and Non's wine. A rather more substantial connection between the two saints can be found in the village of Llan-non in Ceredigion. The parish church there is dedicated to Ffraid, while there is an old and persistent tradition that the village is the place where Non gave birth to Dewi (David).[52] A medieval chapel in Llan-non used to contain 'a stone, 14 inches tall, and 12 inches broad, on which is carved the face of a woman with a child in her arms, traditionally reputed to be that of St. Non with her boy.'[53] Evelyn Lewes wrote that the stone 'has the appearance of great antiquity,' while George Eyre Evans remarked that 'the face of the mother is unlike any other known to me, as intended for the Virgin Mary.'[54]

Discussion of Non has been clouded in recent years by a claim, first made by G.H. Doble and then reiterated by Professor Simon Evans, that she never really existed. It has been suggested that her name 'may originally have been that of a monk, who was a contemporary of David and a companion of his.'[55] At some point in the remote past this male figure (Nonna) underwent a sex-change in the popular mind and turned into Non, Dewi's mother. This theory, based primarily on the derivation of certain church dedications in Cornwall and Brittany, seems to me to be somewhat improbable. The Welsh evidence implies the existence of a cult of a female Non, recognized as Dewi's mother, in Cardiganshire, Pembrokeshire and possibly Carmarthenshire, from a very early period. Elissa Henken has argued that there may have been 'two characters, one a male saint and one David's mother, who both had names which were variations on Non/Nonna/Nonnita, and that in certain areas . . . a confusion between them took place . . .'[56] The work of the Breton hagiographer Per Jakez Hélias supports the idea that Non and her apparent namesake were in fact separate individuals. He notes that Nonn (otherwise known as Nonita, Melaria, Nonne, Nonnite and Mélarie), the mother of Divi (Dewi), is associated in Britanny with Dirinon, Lennon, Lan-Non en Bannalec and Crec'h Nonn en Begard. Nonna (otherwise known as Mo-Onna, Mo-Unna, Monna, Munna and Onna) is an entirely different character: an Irishman who is the patron saint of Penmarc'h, Logonna-Daoulas and Logonna-Quimerch.[57]

111

Rhigyfarch (1056/7-1099), son of Bishop Sulien of St Davids, describes the assault on Non which was said to have led to Dewi's conception:

Sanctus, king of Ceredigion, went to Dyfed, and whilst passing through it, there met him a maiden called Nonita, exceedingly beautiful, a modest virgin. Her the king, inflamed with desire, violated, who, neither before nor after this occasion had any intercourse with any man, but continued in chastity of mind and body, leading a most faithful life; for from this very time of her conceiving, she lived on bread and water only. There, in that very place where she was violated, and where she conceived, lay a small meadow, pleasing to the eye, and by divine favour, laden with heavenly dew. In that meadow, too, at the time of her conception, two large stones, which had not been seen there before, appeared, one at her head, and one at her feet; for the earth, rejoicing in the conceiving, opened its bosom, both in order to preserve the maid's modesty, and also to declare beforehand the significance of her offspring. [58]

That Non should have been violated is not in itself improbable, given the disordered and often brutal nature of the world into which Dewi was born. Women were especially vulnerable in such a society. However the pious verbiage in which Rhigyfarch cloaks his account of the rape, and his concern with Non's 'modesty' rather than her suffering, suggests that he was deliberately attempting to draw parallels between Dewi's mother and the mother of Christ.

Rhigyfarch's Nonita is 'a modest virgin.' He emphasizes that she lived 'in chastity of mind and body,' and that her rape by Sanctus was her only experience of sexual intercourse. Elissa Henken refers to the tradition that the mother of Kentigern (Cyndeyrn) had prayed that she might follow Mary's example, giving birth as a virgin. In fact she too was violated—by a man disguised as a woman. Drawing a parallel with the story of Dewi's conception, Henken comments:

One way of maintaining the innocence of the saint's mother, of providing a father for the child of a woman who does not desire a man, is through rape. . . . These women may have lost the innocence of the body, but not of the mind. [59]

The Llan-non statue of the saint and her child suggests a tendency to see Non and Dewi as a local equivalent of Mary and Jesus. It may also be significant that the fifteenth-century Cardiganshire poet Deio ab Ieuan Du links Mair (Mary) and Non in one of his *cywyddau*.[60]

In connecting Non with the Virgin Mary, Rhigyfarch probably reflects the impact of outside pressures which were trying to enhance the status of celibacy and virginity in the Welsh church during the eleventh century. The Celtic church in Wales had married priests and bishops, many of whom were succeeded by their sons. Even within Welsh monasteries this pattern prevailed. Wendy Davies writes of Welsh religious, 'They may all have considered themselves monks, but if so their vocation did not require celibacy, and their way of life must have had little in common with the popular image of the cloistered monk either now or then in contemporary continental Europe.'[61] By Rhigyfarch's time attempts were being made to make Welsh religious communities conform with the developing practice of the wider church. The growing cult of the Virgin naturally had a part to play in this campaign, which proved only partially successful. The monks became celibate, but throughout the Middle Ages Welsh parish clergy continued to marry, quietly ignoring the decrees of canon law on the subject.[62]

Rhigyfarch is concerned to portray Non as an example of asexual purity. However his description of Dewi's conception and birth also contains motifs which echo pre-Christian ideas. When Dewi is conceived the earth opens up to protect the young woman and to show the importance of her son. The child is born in the midst of a terrible storm which keeps everyone except Non indoors:

> But the place where the mother lay groaning in labour shone with so brilliant a light, that it glistened in God's presence, as if lit by the sun, though it was obscured by clouds.[63]

While giving birth, Non presses so hard on a stone that she is said to have left the imprints of her hands on it. It seems that nature itself sympathizes with Non in her predicament, and this suggests that she has somehow acquired the characteristics of a pre-Christian mother-goddess.

There is other evidence to support this possibility. St Non's Chapel in Pembrokeshire, the traditional location of Dewi's birth and conception, is on a pre-Christian site. The standing stones nearby may be the 'two large stones' which Rhigyfarch claimed had first appeared when Non was raped. Ffynnon Non, the holy well next to the chapel, became famous for its healing properties. Richard Fenton wrote at the beginning of the last century that 'this consecrated spring. . . .still is resorted to for many complaints.' He described how he himself had been dipped in it many times as a child, 'and offerings, however trifling, even of a farthing or a pin, were made after each ablution, and the bottom of the well shone with votive brass.'[64]

Celtic mother-goddesses were concerned with healing, fertility and prosperity. The Pembrokeshire evidence links Non with the first two of these, while the Welsh poetic tradition connects here with the third. The poets associate Non with wine, feasting and generosity. Lewys Môn compares the hospitality of Elin, wife of Owain ap Meurig, with that of Non. Tudur Aled speaks of Non's wealth and compares the wine-cellar of Margret, daughter of Gruffudd ap Rhys, with the abundance of Ffynnon Non.[65] There are hints here and elsewhere of a story about Non which no longer survives. It may have involved her turning water into wine.

Through the centrality of the mother-goddesses the feminine had played an important part in pre-Christian Celtic religion. In their different ways the key figures of Elen Luyddog, Ffraid and Non ensured that this element survived in Celtic Christianity. The popular imagination was able to find ways of identifying all three with Mary, the mother of Christ, thus helping to set the Incarnation at the heart of Welsh Christian spirituality. When at the beginning of the nineteenth century Ann Griffiths, the Methodist farmer's wife from Dolwar Fach, sang her great hymn of wonder at the birth of Christ, she was unconsciously following in a tradition that had its origin with the 'holy mothers' of the early Celtic church in Wales.

NOTES

[1] *Early Welsh Genealogical Tracts,* edited by P.C. Bartrum (Cardiff, 1966), p.9.
[2] *Early Welsh Genealogical Tracts,* p.10.
[3] *Trioedd Ynys Prydein,* p.341.
[4] Geoffrey of Monmouth, *The History of the Kings of Britain,* translated by Lewis Thorpe (Harmondsworth, 1973), p.132.
[5] *Brut Dingestow,* edited by Henry Lewis (Cardiff, 1974), p.69.
[6] J.S.P. Tatlock, *The Legendary History of Britain: Geoffrey of Monmouth's Historia Regum Britanniae and its Early Vernacular Versions* (New York, 1974), p.236; see also the remarks by Rachel Bromwich, *Trioedd Ynys Prydein,* p.341.
[7] *Early Welsh Genealogical Tracts,* p.44.
[8] Evans, *Drych y Prif Oesoedd,* pp.64-5.
[9] Rice Rees, *An Essay on the Welsh Saints* (London, 1836), p.98.
[10] Timothy Barnes, *Constantine and Eusebius* (Cambridge, Massachusetts, 1981), pp.3, 221; *Butler's Lives of the Saints,* edited by Herbert Thurston and Donald Attwater (London, 1956), III, 346.

[11] Ivan D. Margary, *Roman Roads in Britain* (London, 1973), pp.351-7.

[12] *The Mabinogion,* p.85.

[13] *Breuddwyd Maxen,* edited by Ifor Williams (Bangor, 1928), p.xv.

[14] John Davies, *Hanes Cymru* (London, 1990), p.53.

[15] *Trioedd Ynys Prydein,* pp.75-8.

[16] *Early Welsh Genealogical Tracts,* pp.10, 44, 46, 63, 94.

[17] Sulpitius Severus, *Dialogues, Nicene and Post Nicene Fathers,* second series, XI, 41.

[18] E.G. Bowen, *The Settlements of the Celtic Saints in Wales* (Cardiff, 1954), pp.20-1.

[19] Rachel Bromwich, 'The Character of the Early Welsh Tradition' in *Studies in Early British History,* edited by Nora K. Chadwick (Cambridge, 1954), pp.108-9.

[20] Davies, *Hanes Cymru,* p.71; Doble, *Lives of the Welsh Saints,* pp.67, 86.

[21] John Rhys, *Lectures on the Origin and Growth of Religion as illustrated by Celtic Heathendom* (London, 1888), p.161.

[22] *Breuddwyd Maxen,* p.xvi.

[23] Nennius, *British History,* p.24.

[24] Roger Sherman Loomis, *Wales and the Arthurian Legend* (Cardiff, 1956), pp.2-4.

[25] *Trioedd Ynys Prydein,* p.342.

[26] Evans, *Drych y Prif Oesoedd,* p.64.

[27] St. Jerome, *Letters* in *A Select Library of Nicene and Post-Nicene Fathers of the Christian Church,* second series (Grand Rapids, 1983), VI, 64.

[28] *The Liber Landavensis,* pp.339-43.

[29] Barnes, *Constantine and Eusebius,* pp.220-1.

[30] P.W.L. Walker, *Holy City, Holy Places? Christian Attitudes to Jerusalem and the Holy Land in the Fourth Century* (Oxford, 1990), pp.17, 186-7.

[31] Walker, *Holy City, Holy Places?,* pp.127-30, 276-7.

[32] H. Patrick Montague, *The Saints and Martyrs of Ireland* (Gerrards Cross, 1981), pp.20-1.

[33] Proinsias Mac Cana, *Celtic Mythology* (Feltham, 1984), p.34.

[34] Rhys, *Lectures,* pp.74-5; Mac Cana, *Celtic Mythology,* pp.33-4.

[35] Green, *Gods of the Celts,* p.78.

[36] Bowen, *Settlements,* p.97.

[37] Pennar Davies, *Rhwng Chwedl a Chredo* (Cardiff, 1966), p.22; *The Celts,* edited by Sabatino Moscati and others (London, 1991), p.600; Graham Webster, *The British Celts and their Gods under Rome* (London, 1986), p.32.

[38] Webster, *British Celts,* p.32.

[39] Alexander Carmichael, *Carmina Gadelica: Hymns and Incantations* (Edinburgh, 1983), I, 166-8.

[40] Carmichael, *Carmina Gadelica,* I, 166-7.

[41] *Gwaith Iorwerth Fynglwyd,* edited by Howell Ll. Jones and E.I. Rowlands (Cardiff, 1975), p.95.

[42] Lady Gregory, *A Book of Saints and Wonders* (London, 1907), p.11.

[43] Carmichael, *Carmina Gadelica,* III, 156-7.

[44] Carmichael, *Carmina Gadelica,* I, 164-5. There is a different version of the story in *Carmina Gadelica,* III, 154-5.

[45] Carmichael, *Carmina Gadelica,* I, 167.

[46] Carmichael, *Carmina Gadelica,* I, 164, III, 156-7.

[47] *Dictionnaire des Saints bretons,* p.54.

[48] Carmichael, *Carmina Gadelica,* III, 159.

[49] Gregory, *Saints and Wonders,* p.11.

[50] *Early Irish Lyrics: Eighth to Twelfth Century,* edited by Gerard Murphy (Oxford, 1970), p.27.

[51] *Gwaith Iorwerth Fynglwyd,* p.94.

[52] Samuel Rush Meyrick, *The History and Antiquities of the County of Cardigan* (Brecon, 1907), p.263; Baring Gould and Fisher, *Lives,* IV, 22 note.

[53] George Eyre Evans, *Cardiganshire: A Personal Survey of Some of its Antiquities, Chapels, Churches, Fonts, Plate and Registers* (Aberystwyth, 1903), pp.176-7.

[54] Evelyn Lewes, 'Image of St. Non at Llanon, Cardiganshire,' *Archaeologia Cambrensis,* sixth series, XIX (1919), p.533; Evans, *Cardiganshire,* p.177

[55] *The Welsh Life of St David,* edited by D. Simon Evans (Cardiff, 1988), p.27.

[56] Henken, *Traditions of the Welsh Saints,* p.160.

[57] *Dictionnaire des Saints bretons,* pp.288-9.

[58] J.W. James, *Rhigyfarch's Life of St. David* (Cardiff, 1967), pp.30-1.

[59] Henken, *The Welsh Saints,* p.24.

[60] *Gwaith Deio ab Teuan Du a Gwilym ab Ieuan Hen,* edited by A. Eleri Davies (Cardiff, 1992), p.27.

[61] Davies, *Wales in the Early Middle Ages,* p.149.

[62] Glanmor Williams, *Bywyd ac Amserau'r Esgob Richard Davies* (Cardiff, 1953), pp.2-3.

[63] James, *Rhigyfarch's Life,* p.32.

[64] Richard Fenton, *A Historical Tour Through Pembrokeshire* (Brecon, 1903), p.63.

[65] *Gwaith Lewys Môn,* edited by Eurys I. Rowlands (Cardiff, 1975), p.29; *Gwaith Tudur Aled,* I, 199, 166.

Chapter Eight:

COMMUNITIES OF LEARNING,
COMMUNITIES OF LOVE

1. 'An example of religious life, and perfect charity.'

riconium, a small Roman town in what is now south-west Herefordshire, gave its name to the tiny Romano-British kingdom of Erging or Ergyng.[1] It was the seat of a bishop, probably from late Roman times. Wendy Davies has remarked that 'The origin of the Ergyng bishopric is maddeningly obscure.' She wonders why Ariconium should have had a bishop at such an early date.[2] A possible solution may lie with Macsen Wledig's widow, who was said to be a daughter of one of the kings of Erging.

The devotion which Macsen's empress felt for the ascetic bishop Martin of Tours has already been mentioned. Sulpitius Severus graphically describes her obsessive admiration for the aged saint:

> . . . the queen hung upon the lips of Martin, and not inferior to her mentioned in the Gospel, washed the feet of the holy man with tears and wiped them with the hairs of her head. Martin, though no woman had hitherto touched him, could not escape her assiduity, or rather her servile attentions. . . . At last she begs of her husband . . . that all other attendants should be removed from the holy man, and that she alone should wait upon him at meals. Nor could the blessed man refuse too obstinately. His modest entertainment is got up by the hands of the queen; she herself arranges his seat for him; places his table; furnishes him with water for his hands; and serves up the food which she had herself cooked. While he was eating, she, with eyes fixed on the ground, stood motionless at a distance, after the fashion of servants, displaying in all points the modesty and humility of a ministering servant. She herself mixed his drink for him and presented it. When the meal was over, she collected the fragments and crumbs of the bread that had been used, preferring with true faithfulness these remains to imperial banquets.[3]

If, as has been suggested, Martin's fervent devotee returned to Erging after her husband's death in 388, she must have brought many of the saint's ideas and ascetic practices with her. If Ariconium already possessed a bishop she would have ensured that he took Martin as his model. If it did not she would soon have remedied the situation, securing a man as close to her ideal as possible. Erging was thus prepared for its rôle as a cradle of Welsh Celtic Christianity.

The fifth century ran its grim course. The fragile Romano-British kingdoms of the south east collapsed before the invaders from the sea. But Erging was, for the moment, secure. It was too far to the west for the Saxons and too far inland for the Irish pirates. In this sheltered oasis of Romano-British civilization it was possible for a Christianity to develop which retained some of the structures of the old town and villa based religion, while absorbing ascetic tendencies drawn both from Martin of Tours and the Egyptian monasticism whose influence was beginning to filter into Cornwall and south Wales. By the second half of the fifth century 'papa' Dyfrig (Dubricius), bishop of Erging, had emerged as the leader of this movement, which was beginning to spread westwards via the Roman roads.

Dating Dyfrig's life is difficult. John Davies suggests that he lived from c.425 to c.505. Other scholars have argued that he was born much later and died between 532 and 556.[4] In the twelfth century a manuscript was compiled to back the claims of the recently emerged diocese of Llandaff to churches dedicated to Dyfrig and Teilo. This *Liber Landavensis* contained a collection of '*lectiones*' about Dyfrig's life. Although they have been edited, added to and distorted by the Llandaff propagandist, they contain several elements clearly based on Herefordshire traditions about Dyfrig which have some historical value.

They tell us that Dyfrig was born in Erging at Matle or Madle (now Madley) on the River Wye south of Hereford. He was supposed to have been the illegitimate son of the king of Erging's daughter and his miraculous birth took place after her angry father had attempted to kill her.[5] Fenn notes that 'illegitimacy and irregular nativities figure large in the Lives of the Saints.' His view is that Dyfrig was from native Erging stock and that his mother came to be regarded as the 'daughter' of the local king because of her son's close association with the ruler.[6] What is certain is that Dyfrig soon became a significant figure in the little kingdom. His biographer records that 'when he became a man in growth, age, and wisdom, and skilful both in the modern and ancient law, his fame extended throughout all Britain, so that from all parts, not only scholars who were uninstructed came, but also learned men and doctors flocked to him for the sake of study.'[7]

Learning had always had an important place in Celtic society. The Druids had acquired a reputation among the Romans as teachers, one author describing them as *'magistri sapientiae'* ('professors of wisdom'). Caesar mentioned students travelling from Gaul to Britain to study Druidic teachings, and there are references in Irish sources to classes of young noblemen being instructed by a Druid.[8] The school which gathered around Dyfrig seems to have followed this traditional pattern. The *Liber Landavensis* account tells us that the Erging holy man 'retained two thousand clergy for seven successive years at Henllan, on the banks of the Wye, in the literary study of divine and human wisdom; setting forth to them in himself an example of religious life, and perfect charity.' W.J. Rees noted in 1840 that Henllan (Hennlann) was 'Hentland, a parish in Herefordshire, the Church whereof is 4½ miles N.W. by W. from the town of Ross in that county.' There was a tradition that Dyfrig's community had stood 1½ miles from Hentland church 'at a place . . . called Lanfrother, or Lanfrodyr, signifying the Church, or Convent of the Brethren.'[9]

The Llandaff author doubtless exaggerated the size of Dyfrig's monastery, but his description of its function seems to have been correct. After a few years the founder moved his monastic school from Henllan to Mochros (Moccas), not far from his birthplace. Fenn identifies practical and geographical reasons for this transfer: 'a few miles to the East [of Mochros] was the Chester-Caerleon road, and the main road to West Wales was easily accessible to the South.'[10] Wendy Davies has suggested that Dyfrig had a third centre: Llangystennin-garthbenni (Welsh Bicknor), where a monastery certainly existed between 575 and 866. In her opinion Welsh Bicknor was possibly 'the house of Dyfrig'—the saint's episcopal base.[11]

Dyfrig seems to have been a territorial bishop on the Roman pattern: the churches dedicated to him are almost all in Erging.[12] His reputation as a teacher and a holy man, however, gave him a spiritual authority which stretched far beyond that small corner of Herefordshire. The *Liber Landavensis* includes Samson among his disciples and Samson's seventh-century biographer throws some light on Dyfrig's position in the ascetic movement which was developing so rapidly in south Wales.[13] He calls Dyfrig *'papa* Dubricius', underlining the bishop of Erging's status as the father figure of Welsh monasticism. Significantly Dyfrig is responsible for Samson's ordination, his appointment first as cellarer and then as abbot of Caldey, and his consecration as a bishop (probably at Llanilltud Fawr). We are told that it was Dyfrig's custom to spend Lent 'in his own house'

119

(presumably his personal cell) on Caldey Island, which explains his interest in the fledgling community. It is made clear that Dyfrig's authority was supreme there: when the abbot wished to leave the island he had to obtain the bishop's approval. [14]

Canon Doble correctly describes Dyfrig as 'one of the chief figures in the creation of Christian Wales.' [15] Elements from the Romano-British Church, Celtic traditional learning and the ascetic ideas and ideals which had their origins in the Egyptian Desert were creatively combined in the communities which he founded. As a result Welsh Christianity began to develop its own special character. That this included a profound concern for sacred learning can be seen as a part of 'Papa' Dyfrig's legacy to his fellow Welshmen and women. An underlying pattern was becoming established that would reassert itself again and again throughout Welsh history. Gruffydd Jones, the eighteenth-century Rector of Llanddowror, who established circulating schools in an endeavour to save the souls of thousands by teaching them to read the Bible and the Prayer Book Catechism in their own tongue, and the earnest and argumentative members of the adult Sunday Schools which played such a major part in nineteenth and early twentieth-century Welsh life, were, in their own way, direct descendants of the fifth century bishop of Erging.

It is probable that Dyfrig's Erging communities influenced the development of Illtud's great monastic school at Llanilltud Fawr (Llantwit Major) in Glamorgan. [16] Samson's biographer describes Illtud as

> ...of all the Britons the most accomplished in all the Scriptures, namely of the Old and New Testaments, and in those of philosophy [science] of every kind, of geometry namely, and of rhetoric, grammar and arithmetic, and of all the theories of philosophy. And by birth he was a most wise magician, having knowledge of the future. [17]

For E.G. Bowen this passage suggests that 'St. Illtud might have combined in himself elements derived from such diverse sources as the Christian tradition, the Roman aristocracy, and the pagan priesthood.' He regards such cultural fusion as characteristic of south east Wales in the late fifth and early sixth centuries. [18] The area was also open to the same outside ascetic influences which had helped to form Dyfrig's monastic discipline. John Davies has pointed out that Dinas Powys, the seat of the kings of Glywysing, is only eighteen kilometres from Llanilltud. Pottery from Bordeaux, Athens and

Alexandria was being used at the court there during Illtud's lifetime, and with the pottery there doubtless came ideas and possibly books and students as well.[19] This same complex milieu produced a third great teacher, a member of the Glywysing royal family: Cadog of Llancarfan.

2. 'To sail to Ireland in order to study.'

 life of Cadog was written around the year 1100 by Lifris or Lifricus, 'Archdeacon of Gulat Morcant [Glamorgan], and magister of St. Catoc of Lanncaruan'. The author's father was Herwald, the principal bishop in south east Wales during the last half of the eleventh century.[20] Llancarfan was Cadog's principal foundation and Lifris was able to draw on traditions and stories about the saint which had survived there. At the end of the biography he included a collection of fourteen Llancarfan charters, some of them dating from Cadog's lifetime. On the basis of Lifris' work Baring Gould and Fisher tentatively suggest that Cadog was born c.497 and died c.577. He thus belongs to a later generation than Dyfrig and Illtud, and was a contemporary of Gildas, to whom he acted as spiritual guide and confessor.[21]

Cadog's own tutor was Tathan, a former hermit who had founded a monastic school at Caerwent. The teaching he received there seems to have been similar to that offered by Illtud at Llanilltud Fawr: a combination of Christian asceticism and the classics, with Celtic overtones. It may have been at this time that Cadog acquired the enthusiastic and almost fanatical love of learning which appears to have been his most striking personal characteristic. Having outgrown his teacher, he set out to pass on his own knowledge. Lifris gives us a picture of the school which the saint established at Llancarfan with its three buildings: 'a notable little monastery of timber...a refectory, and...a dormitory.' This foundation, we are told, soon became famous:

> ...there eagerly flowed together from various districts of the whole of Britannia very many clerics to saint Cadog like rivers to the sea, that they might attain to imitate his wisdom and practice; for he always welcomed eagerly all, who steadily toiled in the services of God and paid heed to the divine scriptures.[22]

Professor Bowen has pointed out the significance of the geographical position of Llanilltud Fawr and Llancarfan, suggesting that the two monasteries 'probably functioned as channel ports.' He notes that their situation 'hidden away in the lower reaches of small river valleys' offered protection from the pirates who constantly threatened the south Wales sea coast. Other factors, such as convenient access to a major Roman road, and the ease with which the Bristol Channel could be crossed from Llanilltud and Llancarfan, meant that 'With the growing importance of sea traffic as the Dark Ages progressed, these monasteries were well placed to share in the benefits of the important Irish traffic that passed to and from the continent by way of South Wales.'[23] Llancarfan's Irish connection was to play a crucial rôle in the development of Celtic Christianity.

If Lifris is to be believed, Cadog's attraction to Ireland stemmed from his passionate thirst for knowledge. He tells us that 'after a long interval of time...the blessed Cadog spoke to his disciples after this manner, saying, "My brethren most beloved, I now burn with ardent longing to sail to Ireland in order to study".'[24] Tathan (or Meuthi), Cadog's original teacher, had been an Irishman, and this may have influenced his decision. Having made it, he wasted no time, ordering 'a stout skiff, stopped with pitch' and setting out across the Irish Channel in it, accompanied by some of his brethren from Llancarfan.

Arriving speedily among the Irish, he busied himself in eagerly searching out and coming to an agreement as to the most distinguished of the teachers of that nation, that he might be perfectly instructed by him in the knowledge of the seven liberal arts. Thirsting vehemently for the streams of learning, he at last fortunately arrived at the principal monastery of that country, which is called Lismor Muchutu. In that place he was joyfully received by the most learned master of that district and the assembly of all the clergy, who for his sanctity and humility surnamed him with the name of the chief saint of that monastery, to wit, Muchutu, where he remained with that principal teacher for three years, until he succeeded in gaining perfection in all western knowledge. Also in the same city they say a monastery was built in honour of saint Cadog.[25]

When Cadog eventually returned to Wales he brought back with him 'a numerous throng of Irish clergy and of Britons.' They included Macmoil, for whom the saint later established a monastery in Gwent, and Finnian. Cadog's thirst for learning had not yet been slaked, however. Instead of heading for Llancarfan,

122

...when he landed on the British shore, he withdrew with his companions into the parts of Brycheiniog, for he had heard that a celebrated rhetorician, of the name of Bachan, had lately arrived from Italy within those borders. When the blessed Cadog heard the report of his knowledge, he wished not a little to be instructed by him in Latinity after the Roman manner.[26]

Even the discovery that Brycheiniog was suffering from a terrible famine did not dampen Cadog's desire to learn from the visiting teacher. Having sat at Bachan's feet for a while, he finally went back to Llancarfan and rebuilt the monastery, which had fallen into disrepair during his absence.

Father John Ryan, the historian of early Irish monasticism, sees a deep significance in Cadog's visit to Ireland. He identifies Finnian, Cadog's companion and close disciple, as Finnian of Clonard (d.549), the figure who was responsible for the development of the Irish monastic schools. Ryan suggests that 'Finnian, under the influence chiefly of Cadoc, transformed Clonard, founded originally... after the loose Patrician pattern, into a monastery strictly so called.' He notes that

British monasticism...laid stress on study, particularly sacred study, as part of the daily round of duties. Finnian adopted this principle, and the monasteries founded by him and his disciples soon rivalled, if they did not surpass, the schools of secular learning.[27]

The friendship of Finnian and Cadog left its mark in 'the peculiarly British way in which Latin was pronounced in Ireland,' while the monasteries of south east Wales also supplied their Irish counterparts with books.[28] Finnian's most famous pupil was Columba, whose monastery at Iona in Scotland became 'one of the most important centers of learning in northwestern Europe.'[29] If Ryan is right, the impetus for the great Irish intellectual movement which had such a profound effect on Europe from the end of the sixth century came originally from the school of Llancarfan and its founder, with his insatiable desire for knowledge.

One of the charters preserved by Lifris conveys something of the atmosphere of Cadog's community. It dates from the saint's lifetime and refers to the foundation of a monastery by Elli, either at Llanelli in Carmarthenshire or Llanelly in Breconshire. The charter states

123

. . . that Elli, disciple of the blessed Cadog, having been diligently educated by him from an early age and eminently instructed in sacred literature, was the dearest to him of all his disciples. And Elli declared, saying, 'Lo, I have built a church and houses in the name of the Lord, and I and all my successors of the familia of Cadog will be obedient, subject and kindly disposed to the familia of Cadog.'[30]

The monastery is a substitute family for those who, like Elli, have been brought up in it from early childhood. Cadog, the teacher-abbot, becomes the spiritual and intellectual father of the monks. On reaching the stage where he himself is ready to lead a community, Elli goes off to establish one 'in the name of the Lord.' The new community, however, regards itself as an extension of Cadog's family, and its founder remains Cadog's faithful disciple and spiritual son. The pupils of the monastic schools of south east Wales were thus an intellectual and spiritual brotherhood, bound together by a concern for one another, a respect for their teachers, a love of learning and a love of God. In the chaotic circumstances of fifth- and sixth-century Britain they became an unexpected and welcome sign of hope.

3.   'Do the little things. . .'

To the west other Christian communities came into being. They had fewer contacts with Romano-British culture and traditions. As a result they did not stress the importance of sacred learning to the same extent as their brethren in the monastic schools of south east Wales. Instead they seized upon the ascetic principles that had arrived from Egypt and the eastern Mediterranean and made them the basis of their foundations. Rhigyfarch's description of the strict pattern of life in Dewi's monastery in Glyn Rhosyn (now St David's) is probably an accurate portrayal. The monks are shown as engaged in hard physical labour for much of the day:

They place the yoke upon their shoulders; they dig the ground unweariedly with mattocks and spades; they carry in their holy hands hoes and saws for cutting, and provide with their own efforts for all the necessities of the community. Possessions they scorn, the gifts of the wicked they reject, and riches they abhor. There is no bringing in of oxen to have the ploughing done, rather is every one both riches and ox unto himself and the brethren. The work completed, no complaint was heard: no conversation was held beyond that which was necessary, but each one performed the task enjoined with prayer and appropriate meditation.[31]

At Llancarfan Cadog's favourite pupils, Finnian and Macmoil, were excused from helping with the rebuilding of the monastery 'that they might have time for reading.'[32] Dewi would have allowed them no such dispensation.

There was time for study at Tyddewi (Dewi's house) in Glyn Rhosyn, but it came after the work in the fields had been completed. The space before the evening bell rang was reserved for 'reading, writing or praying.' The bell brought this to an abrupt conclusion:

Even if the bell sounded in the ear of any one, when only the tip of a letter or even half the form of the same letter was written, they would rise quickly and leave what they were doing; and so, in silence, without any empty talk or chatter they repair to the church. When they had finished chanting the psalms, during which the heart and the voice were in complete accord, they humble themselves on bended knees until the appearance of the stars in the heavens should bring the day to a close.

This service was followed by a frugal meal of 'bread and herbs seasoned with salt, whilst they quench their thirst with a temperate kind of drink.' 'Tastier food' was provided for 'the sick, those advanced in age, or. . .those wearied by a long journey.' Afterwards Dewi's monks returned to the church for three more hours of 'watching, prayers and genuflexions.' They then slept until cockcrow, when 'they apply themselves to prayer on bended knees, and spend the remainder of the night till morning without sleep.' Rhigyfarch tells us that they held all things in common: 'whosoever should say 'my book' or 'my anything else' would be straightway subjected to a severe penance.' The monks' clothing was basic: 'of mean quality, mainly skins.'[33]

Dewi, described by Rhigyfarch as 'the father' of the community dedicated to this demanding pattern of life, probably died in the year 589.[34] His roots seem to have been in central Ceredigion and he began his education at the little monastery of Henfynyw, near Aberaeron, under the wing of the local bishop Guistilianus. From there he travelled to north Carmarthenshire to be taught by Peulin (Paulinus), probably at Llanddeusant, before founding his own monastic settlement at Glyn Rhosyn.[35] Dewi's community became the focus of a missionary movement which established churches throughout south west Wales.

This area was the scene of two major and possibly interconnected conflicts during Dewi's lifetime. In the fifth and sixth centuries a large area of south Cardiganshire, north Pembrokeshire and west Carmarthenshire was settled by Irish invaders. In some parts they even appear to have assumed political control.These incomers were Goidelic-speaking 'Q Celts' as opposed to the Brythonic 'P Celts' of Wales. Their incursion threatened the survival of Welsh culture in Dyfed. In Rhigyfarch's life of Dewi they are represented by the Irish chieftain Baia, who does everything in his power to prevent the establishment of the monastery at Glyn Rhosyn. The Welsh-speaking churches founded by Dewi and his followers counteracted the effects of the Irish influx. As well as fulfilling a religious function, they provided the Welsh with a cultural and linguistic base. [36]

It may have been this rôle of upholding and preserving Welsh culture in the west at a time when its future was threatened that earned Dewi the special status which would eventually lead to his general acceptance as patron saint of Wales. He had apparently achieved this symbolic position by 930 when the prophetic poem *'Armes Prydein'* was composed to rally the Welsh against the English king Athelstan. It contains a reference to *'lluman glan Dewi'* ('the holy banner of Dewi') being raised as the standard of the Welsh armies. [37] That the earlier struggle against the Irish may have led to some violent clashes is suggested by an inscription which has survived (although damaged during the last century) in the church founded by Dewi at Llanddewi Brefi in Cardiganshire. It dates from between 600 and 650, not long after Dewi's death, and is generally interpreted as reading 'Here lie the remains of Idnerth son of Jacob, who was killed while defending the church of holy David from being despoiled.' [38]

Llanddewi Brefi also played an important part in the second conflict: the theological battle against Pelagianism. Back in 429 Germanus of Auxerre had visited the fragile Romano-British community in south east Britain in an attempt to refute Pelagian ideas. The 'British heresy' lingered on, however, and seems to have found a following among the Irish immigrants in west Wales. A study of early Christian memorial formulae in Wales has shown that inscriptions reflecting Pelagian ideas were widespread in west Wales during Dewi's lifetime. Many of them were carved bilingually in Latin and Old Irish (using the ogham script). It thus seems likely that religious and racial/tribal divisions in west Wales had begun to

126

coincide. Dewi became recognized as the leader of those who opposed the Pelagians. At a synod held at Llanddewi Brefi he ensured that his fellow Welshmen showed their firm support for the orthodox faith.[39]

Professor Bowen has emphasized the essentially tribal nature of the Synod of Brefi. He reminds us that Dewi was

> ...a tribal bishop who wore rough clothing, possibly of animal skins, and carried a large branch from the woods rather than a crosier, and may well have been bareheaded and barefooted. He carried a bell which he called 'Bangu', 'the dear loud one', which possessed magical powers.[40]

Rhigyfarch tried to depict this rough-and-ready figure as a powerful territorial archbishop on the Roman pattern, whose authority would be recognized and understood by Anglo-Norman prelates. His life of Dewi was probably written as an attempt to defend the integrity and independence of the diocese of St Davids against Anselm, the newly-consecrated Archbishop of Canterbury, who was trying to assert his jurisdiction over the Welsh.[41] Two and a half centuries later an anchorite, whose cell was at Llanddewi Brefi, produced a shorter life of Dewi in Welsh for the use of the local community. Professor Simon Evans has underlined the special characteristics of the anchorite's work, commenting that 'there is in the Welsh *Life* generally emphasis on David's simple goodness and godliness, on his humility and devotion, on his miracles, to the exclusion of other aspects.'[42]

One of the most significant differences between the two lives is in their account of Dewi's final message to his followers. Rhigyfarch records the saint as saying *'Fratres mei, perseuerate in his quę a me didicistis et uidistis'* ('My brethren, persevere in those things which you have learned from me and have seen in me').[43] The anchorite's version is longer: *'Arglwydi, vrodyr a chwioryd, bydwch lawen a chedwch awch ffyd a'ch cret, a gwnewch y petheu bychein a glywsawch ac a welsawch y gennyf i'* ('Lords, brothers and sisters, be happy and keep your faith and your belief, and do the little things that you have heard and seen me do').[44] The second message is the one which has embedded itself in the heart of Welsh Christian tradition. It may represent a genuine saying of Dewi's that had been preserved by his Cardiganshire followers. Certainly it reflects the character and quality of the religious life of the churches established by Dewi throughout south west Wales. It is addressed not just to a group of monks but to an all-embracing Christian community ('Lords, brothers and sisters'). It stresses joy, faith and belief and above all 'the little things'—the small but all-

127

important actions which form the foundation of everyday Christian living. This aspect of Dewi's spirituality does appear elsewhere in Rhigyfarch's picture of the saint. He describes Dewi's daily life as a combination of spiritual devotion and acts of charity and kindness which are not solely confined to the members of his own community:

> The whole of the day he spent, inflexibly and unweariedly, in teaching, praying, genuflecting and in care for the brethren; also in feeding a multitude of orphans, wards, widows, needy, sick, feeble and pilgrims: so he began; so he continued; so he ended. [45]

The memory of Dewi's strict asceticism survived throughout the Middle Ages. Lewys Glyn Cothi, writing about him in the fifteenth century, remarked:

> *Bara gymerth a berwr,*
> *Neu ddŵr afonydd oerion;*
> *Ac o'r rhawn, gwisg ar ei hyd,*
> *A phenyd ar lan ffynnon.* [46]

('He took bread and cress, or water from cold rivers; and wore a full-length horse-hair garment, and did penance beside a spring.')

But Dewi's lasting influence on Welsh Christianity did not come from this harsher side of his spirituality. His emphasis on the 'little things' was to have a far more permanent impact on the people of west Wales. In any community apparently insignificant acts of habitual kindness and self-forgetfulness which display a fundamental respect and love for others can generate stability, unity and wholeness. On the other hand, acts of unkindness or contempt, however superficially trivial, can quickly lead to the disintegration of a society as feuds develop and are fuelled by an unwillingness to forgive.

Dewi's legacy to the tribal groups and extended families who formed his churches was a set of values which can still be discerned in some of the Welsh-speaking rural communities of west Wales. They include such qualities as *'parch'* ('respect'—the sort of respect that can only be earned by showing genuine respect for others) and *'bod yn isel'* ('being lowly'—in the sense of not being puffed-up, arrogant or proud) and a realization of the importance of being *'cartrefol'* ('at home') both with God and our neighbours. An emphasis on *'perthyn'* ('belonging') was something which these tribal groups already possessed and which developed into a sense of being related to God through the saint who had brought them as a community into the

Christian fold. The tribe or group of families whose life and worship was centred on a particular church would become 'Dewi's people', 'Teilo's people' or 'Padarn's people', taking their name either from the founder of the church itself or of the founder of the community of which he was a part. Gradually the attempt was made to create a network of Christian communities based on love of God and love of neighbour and held together by a common faith.

The most powerful modern interpretation of Dewi's spirituality is contained in Gwenallt's poem to the saint:

Gwelais Ddewi yn rhodio o sir i sir fel sipsi Duw
Â'r Efengyl a'r Allor ganddo yn ei garafán;
A dyfod atom i'r Colegau a'r ysgolion
I ddangos inni beth yw diben dysg.
Disgynnodd i waelod pwll glo gyda'r glowyr
A bwrw golau ei lamp gall ar y talcen;
Gwisgo ar staeds y gwaith dur y sbectol a'r crys bach glas
A dangos y Cristion yn cael ei buro fel metel yn y ffwrnais;
Ac arwain y werin ddiwydiannol i'w Eglwys amharchus.
Cariodd ei Eglwys i bobman
Fel corff, a hwnnw yn fywyd, ymennydd ac ewyllys
A wnâi bethau bach a mawr.
Daeth â'r Eglwys i'n cartrefi,
Rhoi'r Llestri Santaidd ar ford y gegin,
A chael bara o'r pantri a gwin sâl o'r seler,
A sefyll y tu ôl i'r bwrdd fel tramp
Rhag iddo guddio rhagom ryfeddod yr Aberth.
Ac wedi'r Cymun cawsom sgwrs wrth y tân,
A soniodd ef wrthym am Drefn naturiol Duw,
Y person, y teulu, y genedl a'r gymdeithas o genhedloedd,
A'r Groes yn ein cadw rhag troi un ohonynt yn dduw. [47]

('I saw Dewi strolling from county to county like God's gypsy, with the Gospel and the Altar in his caravan; and coming to us in the Colleges and schools to show us what is the purpose of learning. He went down to the bottom of the pit with the miners and cast the light of his wise lamp on the coal-face; on the platform of the steel works he put on the goggles and the little blue shirt and showed the Christian being purified like metal in the furnace; and led the proletariat to his unrespectable Church. He carried his Church everywhere as a body, life, brain and will that did little and great things. He brought the Church to our homes, and took bread from the pantry and bad wine from the cellar, and stood behind the table like a tramp so as not to hide the wonder of the Sacrifice from us. And after the Communion we chatted by the fireside, and he talked to us about God's natural order, the person, the family, the nation and the society of nations, and the Cross keeping us from turning any one of them into a god.')

By bringing God into the heart of daily life, *'y cartref a'r aelwyd'* ('the home and the hearth'), Dewi and his followers sought to transform that life. They left an impression that is still discernable in the values and aspirations of some of the Welsh-speaking rural communities of west Wales, even in their present beleaguered and threatened position. After a time of invasions that brought chaos, fear and despair, their small communities of love offered a possible pattern for a kinder future: a glimpse of the Kingdom of God.

NOTES

[1] R.W.D. Fenn, 'St. Dyfrig and Christianity in South East Wales,' *Province*, XI (1960), p.25.
[2] Wendy Davies, *An Early Welsh Microcosm: Studies in the Llandaff Charters* (London, 1978), p.157.
[3] Sulpitius, *Dialogues*, p.41.
[4] Davies, *Hanes Cymru*, p.71; Doble, *Lives of the Welsh Saints*, p.59, note 8.
[5] *Liber Landavensis*, p.323.
[6] Fenn, 'St. Dyfrig and Christianity,' pp.24-5.
[7] *Liber Landavensis*, p.324.
[8] Stuart Piggott, *The Druids* (London, 1985), pp.108-9.
[9] *Liber Landavensis*, pp.324-5 and note.
[10] Fenn, 'St. Dyfrig and Christianity,' p.61.
[11] Davies, *Early Welsh Microcosm*, pp.123-4, 134, 145, 157-8. Baring Gould and Fisher, *Lives*, II, 379, refer to Welsh Bicknor as 'a branch establishment' of Dyfrig's.
[12] Davies, *Early Welsh Microcosm*, p.144; Bowen, *Settlements*, p.36.
[13] *Liber Landavensis*, p.324.
[14] Taylor, *Life of St. Samson*, pp.19-20, 37-9, 44-5.
[15] Doble, *Lives of the Welsh Saints*, p.86.
[16] Fenn, 'St. Dyfrig and Christianity,' pp.62, 65.
[17] Taylor, *Life of St. Samson*, p.14.
[18] Bowen, *Settlements*, p.45.
[19] Davies, *Hanes Cymru*, pp.72-3.
[20] Wade-Evans, *Vitae*, p.xi.
[21] Baring Gould and Fisher, *Lives*, II, 37; Wade-Evans, *Vitae*, p.97.
[22] Wade-Evans, *Vitae*, pp.45, 47.
[23] Bowen, *Settlements*, p.45.
[24] Wade-Evans, *Vitae*, p.47.
[25] Wade-Evans, *Vitae*, p.49.
[26] Wade-Evans, *Vitae*, pp.49, 129.

[27] John Ryan, *Irish Monasticism: Origins and Early Development* (London, 1931), pp.115-16.

[28] Ryan, *Irish Monasticism,* p.380.

[29] Ian Finlay, *Columba* (London, 1979), pp.62-3; *The Celts,* pp.623-4.

[30] Wade-Evans, *Vitae,* pp. 131, 133.

[31] James, *Rhigyfarch's Life,* p.36.

[32] Wade-Evans, *Vitae,* p.53.

[33] James, *Rhigyfarch's Life,* pp.36-7.

[34] *Dictionary of Welsh Biography,* p.107.

[35] E.G. Bowen, *The Saint David of History. Dewi Sant: Our Founder Saint* (Aberystwyth, 1982), pp.11-14; E.G. Bowen, *Dewi Sant: Saint David* (Cardiff, 1983), pp.18-23, 28-9; D. Ben Rees, *Hanes Plwyf Llanddewi Brefi* (Llanddewi Brefi, 1984), p.22.

[36] Davies, *Wales in the Early Middle Ages,* pp.88-9, 95; Bowen, *Dewi Sant,* pp.34-7; James, *Rhigyfarch's Life,* pp.34-5.

[37] *Armes Prydein o Lyfr Taliesin,* edited by Ifor Williams (Cardiff, 1955), pp.xvi-xvii, 5, 129.

[38] Rees, *Hanes Plwyf Llanddewi Brefi,* pp.22-5.

[39] Bowen, *Saint David of History,* pp.23-7; Bowen, *Dewi Sant,* pp.62-7; James, *Rhigyfarch's Life,* pp.43-5.

[40] Bowen, *Dewi Sant,* p.71.

[41] James, *Rhigyfarch's Life,* p.xi.

[42] *Welsh Life of St David,* p.lii.

[43] James, *Rhigyfarch's Life,* pp.26, 47.

[44] *Buched Dewi,* edited by D. Simon Evans (Cardiff, 1965), p.21.

[45] James, *Rhigyfarch's Life,* p.38.

[46] *Lewys Glyn Cothi (Detholiad),* edited by E.D. Jones (Cardiff, 1984), p.101.

[47] D. Gwenallt Jones, *Eples* (Llandysul, 1951), pp.63-4.

131

Chapter Nine:

THE UNEXPECTED GLORY

1.   'Christ gave him an honourable altar from heaven...'

he focus of every Celtic Christian community in Wales was
the altar. This is made clear in David James' description of
the *'clas'* (monastic settlement) at Glyn Rhosyn in Dewi's
time:

> Inside....a wattled circular palisade surrounding the wattled huts
> of monks was a wooden church, small as Celtic churches were,
> which housed the altar rather than the community at worship.
> Around was the land this community farmed, and the district they
> accepted into their spiritual care. [1]

The Celtic church which has been excavated at Ynys Seiriol (Priestholm)
off the coast of Anglesey supports this picture. It was only five foot
square, providing shelter for the altar and the Eucharistic celebrant.
A Llancarfan charter, dating from Cadog's lifetime, mentions that
the saint 'built a church for Macmoil, his disciple, and secured it with
a rampart and built an altar in the same.' [2] There is an example of a
Celtic altar, with three crosses carved into the stone, in Llanllwni
Church at Maesycrugiau in north Carmarthenshire.

Christian altars seem to have been credited with many of the
strange properties ascribed to sacred stones by the pagan Celts. Often
an altar was regarded as the possession of a particular saint, acquiring
a reputation for those same mysterious powers which were also
associated with the saints' staffs, handbells and holy books. [3]
According to Rhigyfarch, the patriarch of Jerusalem sent Dewi four
gifts after the Welshman had made a pilgrimage there. They included
'a consecrated altar on which he consecrated the Lord's Body, which,
potent with many miracles, has never been seen by men since its
bishop's death, but lies hidden, concealed by coverings of skins.' [4] In
the account of the pilgrimage included in the *Liber Landavensis* the
altar is said to have been given to Dewi because he celebrated the
Eucharist more cheerfully than Teilo and Padarn, his two
companions. No one knew the material out of which it was made. [5] A
somewhat different tradition is recorded in a poem written by

Gwynfardd Brycheiniog in the late twelfth century. He says that Dewi's altar was sent from heaven and that no one was able to look at it.[6]

One of the most famous altars in early Welsh tradition is that which belonged to Carannog. Two lives of this Cardiganshire saint survive, both of them dating from the early twelfth century.[7] In the earliest of the two we are told that 'Christ gave him an honourable altar from heaven, the colour of which no one fathomed.' This remarkable stone could float on water, as Carannog found when he threw it into the estuary of the Severn. Indeed it is said that the altar 'preceded him whither God wished him to go.' At one point the altar fell into the hands of king Arthur, who tried to convert it into an ordinary table, only to find that 'whatever was placed upon it was thrown to a distance.' Arthur gave Carannog land for a church in recompense. Not long afterwards Carannog was told by a voice from heaven to throw the altar in the sea again. Arthur enquired where it had landed and granted the spot to the saint to build another church.[8]

This curious legend developed because the relatively small number of churches dedicated to Carannog are scattered between west Wales, Cornwall (where he is known as Carantoc), Brittany (where he becomes Carantec) and Ireland (where he is probably Cairnach, patron of a church in County Meath).[9] However the prominence given to the altar in the tradition is a reminder, not only of the special powers with which such stones were credited, but also of its central importance in the foundation of any church. Carannog's altar was presumably thought to be at Llangrannog in Cardiganshire, the centre of his cult. The story that it had once skimmed across the waves to Cornwall and Brittany was a colourful attempt to explain the existence of the other far-flung outposts devoted to him.

Both Carannog and Dewi (in Gwynfardd Brycheiniog's version of the tradition) were said to have received their altars from heaven. This belief reflects a consciousness that the celebration of the Eucharist was a point of contact between heaven and earth, when by a miracle of grace the body and blood of Christ became present on the sacred stone through the prayers of a holy man. The saints themselves were transfigured as they performed this action. Rhigyfarch describes how Dewi 'overflowing with daily fountains of tears, and fragrant with sweet-smelling offerings of prayers, and radiant with a twofold flame of charity, consecrated with pure hands the due oblation of the Lord's Body.'[10] Samson's Breton biographer, after describing how the saint was consecrated bishop says

... as he was singing Mass on the same day in the presence of them all, it was apparent to Father Dubricius and to two distinguished monks that there proceeded from his nostrils as it had been fire. And, what is greater than all these things, from that day when he became a presbyter until his happy death, when he sang Mass, the angels of God ever became holy ministers of the altar and of sacrifice along with him, and often broke the oblation with their hands though he alone saw it. [11]

Dewi's radiance 'with a twofold flame of charity' and the fire which Dyfrig and his companions saw when Samson consecrated the Eucharist for the first time reflect an idea about the way in which holiness is revealed which has its origins in the Christian East. Among the sayings of the Egyptian Desert Fathers, who provided the main inspiration for the ascetic movement in the Celtic lands, was the advice of the influential hermit Abba Joseph of Panephysis to Abba Lot, a simple Coptic monk:

Abba Joseph said to Abba Lot, 'You cannot become a monk unless you become like a consuming fire.'
Abba Lot went to see Abba Joseph and said to him, 'Abba, as far as I can I say my little office, I fast a little, I pray and meditate, I live in peace and as far as I can I purify my thoughts. What else can I do?' Then the old man stood up and stretched his hands towards heaven. His fingers became like ten lamps of fire and he said to him, 'If you will, you can become all flame.' [12]

The descriptions of Dewi and Samson at the altar suggest that they had attained this degree of spiritual perfection. The reference to angels acting as concelebrants with Samson may also stem from eastern Christian beliefs. [13]

Just as the altar was the physical focal point of the Celtic *clas,* the Eucharist stood at the centre of its devotional life, being celebrated on Sundays, saints' days and other special occasions. [14] Even in post-Reformation Welsh spirituality it has continued to play an important (if usually unacknowledged) rôle. It was a feeling of having taken communion unworthily which led to the conversion of Howel Harris (1714-73), one of the two great founders of Welsh Methodism. Reading a Welsh translation of Bishop Lewis Bayly's *Practice of Piety* convinced him that his sins could be forgiven at Holy Communion if he went forward to receive the sacrament believing that such forgiveness was possible. On Whitsunday 1735 he went to Talgarth church, feeling anxious and uncertain. During the Communion he concentrated on the figure of Christ, bleeding on the cross. Suddenly he knew that he was forgiven. His burden of guilt and worry disappeared and he was overwhelmed with a feeling of joy and relief. [15]

The Eucharist also played a central part in the ministry of the other important Welsh Methodist leader, Daniel Rowland of Llangeitho (1713-90). In the eighteenth century Communion was only administered three times a year in most Anglican churches. Rowland began a monthly celebration of the sacrament in Llangeitho. On Communion Sundays people flocked to the little Cardiganshire village to listen to the great preacher and receive the sacrament from his hand. Rowland's first biographer noted that

> I have heard from a godly old servant of Rowland's that there were on occasions people from every county in Wales in Llangeitho, and that sometimes at the end of the month there were not less than twelve to fifteen hundred or more there, taking communion: they were normally from a thousand to twelve hundred. He was able to make a good estimate of their number, because he prepared the communion bread. [16]

The Anglican priest and poet Nicander (Morris Williams, 1809-74) included a poem in his collection *Y Flwyddyn Eglwysig* which seems to combine the Eucharistic experience of the Celtic saints with that of Howel Harris and the early Welsh Methodists. In a shortened and slightly revised version it has become one of the best-loved hymns of the Church in Wales:

> *Gyda'r saint anturiais nesu*
> *Dan fy maich at Allor Duw:*
> *Bwrdd i borthi'r tlawd newynog,*
> *Bwrdd i nerthu'r egwan yw;*
> *Cefais yno megis gyffwrdd*
> *Corph drylliedig Iesu Glân,*
> *Yn y fan fe doddai 'nghalon*
> *Fel y cwyr o flaen y tân.* [17]

('With the saints I ventured to approach God's Altar, bearing my burden. It is a table to feed the starving poor, it is a table to strengthen the weak. There I, as it were, touched the broken body of holy Jesus. Suddenly my heart melted like wax before the fire.')

Nicander's 'burden' included the religious doubts and uncertainties that were characteristic of his time. Like Dewi, Samson and Carannog in an earlier age of insecurity, he experienced the present reality of God at the moment of Communion, and his faith and trust and hope were renewed.

2.   'Padarn...was an excellent singer.'

Gwenallt has written movingly of the way in which '*yr hen emynau*' ('the old hymns') shaped his spiritual life, as they did that of several generations of Welsh-speaking Christians:

> *Buont yn canu uwch fy nghrud,*
> *Uwchben fy machgendod a'm hieuenctid,*
> *Fel côr o adar Cristionogol:*
> *Hwynt-hwy â'u cân oedd yn cario Calfaria*
> *A'r Groes i ganol y gweithfeydd;*
> *Bethlehem a'r crud i ganol y tipiau;*
> *Y bedd gwag i blith y gwagenni,*
> *A dwyn afon yr Iorddonen heb fitrel yn ei dûr.*

('They sang over my cradle, above my boyhood and my youth, like a choir of Christian birds: they and their song carried Calvary and the Cross into the midst of the factories; Bethlehem and the crib into the midst of the coal-tips; the empty grave amongst the wagons, and brought the river Jordan without vitriol in its water.')

He describes how he had tried to chase these 'Christian birds' away with his scientific gun and his materialistic cudgel. Nevertheless, without him being conscious of it, they had stubbornly continued to sing '*O dan rhiniog y rheswm a charreg-drws y deall*' ('Under the threshold of reason and the door-step of understanding').

> *A phan ddaeth y goleuni yn ôl i'r goedwig*
> *Esgynasant o blith y gwraidd i'r canghennau a'r brig*
> *I ganu eilwaith, a'u cân wedi aeddfedu yn y nos:*
> *Dwyn y crud, y Groes, y bedd gwag a'r Pentecost*
> *Yn ôl o'r newydd, yn danbaid newydd...* [18]

('And when the light came back to the forest they flew up from amongst the roots to the branches and the tree-tops to sing again, and their song had matured in the night: carrying the crib, the Cross, the empty grave and Pentecost back again, fierily new...')

Gwenallt was aware of the spiritual power of the classic Welsh hymns which reflected the profound religious experience of such writers as William Williams (Pantycelyn), Dafydd Jones, Morgan Rhys and Ann Griffiths. When he rediscovered the Christian faith the verses which had been familiar since his childhood acquired a new depth of meaning: 'their song had matured in the night.' Given the rôle that such hymns have played in the religious life of Wales during the past two and a half centuries it is worth looking to see if there are any remote echoes of a similar force at work in the devotion and worship of the Celtic church in Wales.

Padarn, Dewi and Teilo, the three saints who were the principal founders of churches in west Wales, became known as the *'Trisant'*. They were also described as the 'Three Blessed Visitors of the Island of Britain.'[19] The most celebrated tradition connecting the three tells of their pilgrimage to Jerusalem. Different versions of it developed, each extolling the virtue of the saint who was patron of the author's church. The account in the life of Teilo included in the *Liber Landavensis* uses the story to play off its subject's humility against the supposed pride of his two companions. It also, however, records an interesting detail about Padarn. 'Three valuable presents. . . .such as suited each person' were given to the pilgrims, and we are told that 'Padarn had a staff, and a choral cap, made of valuable silk, because they observed that he was an excellent singer.'[20] This incident has earned Padarn the reputation of being the most musical of the Welsh saints. The episode is unlikely to have any reliable historical basis. Baring Gould and Fisher dismiss the pilgrimage as 'a deliberate fabrication of Welsh ecclesiastics in the twelfth century.'[21] Nevertheless it does seem to indicate the importance of choral singing in the Welsh church.

In his study of Celtic liturgy F.E. Warren noted that 'The services of the Celtic Church, both at the altar and in the choir, were choral.' He suggested that the style of singing used came from the Eastern churches by way of Gaul, arriving in Britain in the fifth century.[22] The surviving evidence is rather thin on the ground, but it does suggest that choral singing played an important part in the pattern of worship of Welsh monastic communities. Thus one of the early Llancarfan charters dating from Cadog's lifetime refers to 'giving of thanks and rejoicing, prayers and spiritual hymns.'[23] The Breton life of Samson mentions a deacon who 'had sung the Gospel and prayer.' It also refers to Samson habitually singing Mass with three brothers and to his singing Mass before a large congregation on the day that he was consecrated bishop.[24] Chanting of psalms formed a central part of the worship of Dewi's monastery according to Rhigyfarch. Dewi's biographer was the son of a native of Llanbadarn Fawr, the community founded by Padarn. His personal psalter, a product of the Llanbadarn monastic *scriptorium,* has survived. Written by a scribe named Ithael, it was decorated in the Irish style by Rhigyfarch's brother Ieuan.[25]

Rhigyfarch tells us that Dewi's monks sang hymns at Matins. Sadly, the hymns themselves have not survived. Nor have the service books of the early Welsh church. The only known Welsh antiphonal dates from the fourteenth century. It contains a Latin rhymed office of St David which may have been composed either around the year 1224, during the episcopate of Iorwerth, a Welshman who became a reforming bishop of St Davids, or about 1285, when Thomas Bek was in charge of the see.[26] Glanmor Williams has written that 'The existence of a virile and rigorous school of musicianship in Wales during the Middle Ages seems to be firmly established.'[27] Presumably such a school had developed from beginnings during the Celtic period.

While the early Welsh material has all been lost, an abundance of early Irish hymns are extant. Initially they were written in Latin, but by the sixth or seventh century they had begun to be composed in the vernacular as well.[28] Perhaps the nearest that we can get to them in Welsh are a group of simple poems of praise to God in the thirteenth-century *Llyfr Du Caerfyrddin.* It has been suggested that they are the work of a single writer during the twelth century. Meirion Pennar has commented, however, that they 'seem to belong to the tradition in Celtic lands of hermit poetry—incandescent pieces created out in the open, in the God-created wild, much like their counterparts in Ireland.'[29]

One of these poems in particular seems to convey the atmosphere of early Welsh Christian worship at its most all-encompassingly enthusiastic:

> *Gogonedauc argluit hanpich guell.*
> *Ath uendicco de egluis. a chagell.*
> *A. kagell. ac egluis.*
> *A. vastad. a diffuis.*
> *A. teir finhuan yssit.*
> *Due uch guint. ac vn uch eluit.*
> *A. yr isgaud ar dit.*
> *A. siric a perwit.*

Ath uendiguis te awraham pen fit.
A. vuchet tragiuit.
A. adar a guenen.
A. attpaur. a dien.
Ath uendigus te aron a moesen.
A. vascul a femen.
A. seithnieu a ser.
A. awir. ac ether.
A. llevreu a llyther.
A piscaud in hydiruer.
A. kywid. a gueithred.
A. tyuvod a thydued.
A. y saul da digoned.
Ath uendigaf de argluit gogoned.
Gogonedauc. a. h. G. [30]

('Hail, glorious Lord! May church and chancel praise you. May chancel and church praise you. May valley floor and mountain side praise you. May the three well-springs, two above the wind and one above the earth, praise you. May night and day praise you. May silk and fruit-tree praise you. Abraham, founder of the faith, praised you. May eternal life praise you. May birds and bees praise you. May after-grass and fresh shoots praise you. Aaron and Moses praised you. May male and female praise you. May the seven days and the stars praise you. May the air and the upper atmosphere praise you. May books and letters praise you. May fishes in the river praise you. May thought and action praise you. May sand and soil praise you. May all the good that has been done praise you. I praise you, Lord of glory! Hail, glorious Lord!')

This beautiful Celtic *Benedicite,* with its praise tumbling forth in an ecstatic appreciation of God's all-embracing glory, reflects the extraordinary sense of joy and rejoicing ('*gorfoleddu*' as the eighteenth-century Methodists called it) which has so often played a part in Welsh religious history. It stems from the often quite unexpected discovery that God's love, once realized, has the potential to transform the apparent chaos and confusion of creation into a harmonious hymn of blessing.

3. 'He did bestowe much of his tyme in prayers...'

A pillar-cross at Penmon in the Dindaethwy district of Anglesey, probably dating from the late tenth century, includes a scene showing St Antony of Egypt being tempted in the desert. The robed saint is surrounded by animal-headed demons.[31] Antony's spiritual warfare against the powers of darkness in his lonely solitude was powerfully described by Athanasius in his life of the founder of the monastic movement, a book which greatly influenced ascetics in the Celtic lands. His experiences were seen as providing a pattern for all those who embarked on a life of prayer. As Derwas Chitty has emphasized, the Desert Fathers taught that the aim of such a life was 'the recovery of Adam's condition before the Fall.'[32] They saw the fallen human state as profoundly unnatural and regarded the purpose of human existence as the attempt to restore men and women to the image and likeness of God, who is love.

It is especially significant that a cross depicting Antony should have been erected at Penmon. The original church there was a small rectangular chapel built over a holy well, with an oval-shaped hut next to it. It had been built by Seiriol, who probably settled there in the first half of the sixth century. Nearby are the remains of a large cluster of hut-groups, possibly a tribal centre which the saint may have served.[33] Seiriol was also responsible for the beginnings of the community of ascetics on nearby Ynys Lannog or Ynys Seiriol (also known as Priestholm or Puffin Island). These 'hermits, who live in the service of God by the labour of their hands,' were still there when Giraldus Cambrensis visited Anglesey in 1188. Professor Bowen has described the remains of their hermitage, near the centre of the island. A boundary wall enclosed some three-quarters of an acre around the church. Inside it were the remains of three or four rectangular cells and some other enclosures. Three small rectangular fields had been closed in outside the main wall. The original church was tiny. Bowen comments that 'the whole arrangement resembles a small farm or villa.'[34]

Seiriol appears to have combined the rôles of tribal holy man and ascetic solitary. Ynys Seiriol was not his only refuge from the world. Sir John Wynn of Gwydir (1553-1627) recorded that

This Seiriol hadd also an hermitage at Penmen Mawr, and there hadd a chappell where he did bestowe much of his tyme in prayers, the place beynge then an uncouth desarte and unfrequented rocke,

140

and unaccessible both in regard of the steepness of the rocke and of the deseartness of the wilderness. There beynge so thicke of wood that a man havynge once entered thereinto coulde hardly behoulde or see skye or ffirmament. . . [35]

There is evidence that other Welsh saints similarly used to withdraw from their communities for periods of private prayer and spiritual struggle. Thus Samson spent some time as a hermit in 'a very spacious and very lonely cave, and its mouth being situated towards the east, he embraced it affectionately as though it had been given by God for a dwelling.'[36] Shorter retreats often took place in Lent in imitation of the forty days which Christ spent in the wilderness. It was apparently Dyfrig's custom to spend Lent on Caldey Island, while Cadog spent the penitential season either on Barry Island or Ynys Echni (Flatholm). Gildas spent a longer period as a hermit on Ynys Echni. As well as passing his time there in prayer, he also wrote a mass book, which he gave to Cadog.[37]

Lifris says that Gildas presented the volume to Cadog 'when he was his confessor.' This leads Father Ryan to describe the older man as probably having acted as 'a spiritual director or "soul friend"' to Gildas.[38] The practice of turning for spiritual guidance either to an older or more experienced teacher or to a friend who was undertaking the same pilgrimage of prayer had come from the Desert Fathers. One the most famous of such spiritual friendships in Welsh tradition was said to have been between Seiriol and Cybi:

> Seiriol Wyn a Chybi Felyn—
> Cyfarfyddant, fel mae'r sôn,
> Beunydd wrth ffynhonnau Clorach
> Yng nghanolbarth Môn.[39]

('Fair Seiriol and Tawny Cybi met, as it is said, daily by the springs of Clorach in the centre of Anglesey.')

Unfortunately Sir J.E. Lloyd dismisses this 'picturesque legend' as 'a bit of modern folk-lore.'[40]

Spiritual guidance acquired a new dimension in Wales and Ireland with the development of private confession and penance, as opposed to the public penance practised among early Christians. Kathleen Hughes remarks that

> Confession and penance were the 'medicine for souls'. They were intended to heal the hurt which a man did by his sin; primarily the

hurt to himself, and also the hurt to society. The confessor was a 'soul-friend': *anm-chara* is his name in Irish. His job was to apply the appropriate cure to the soul's disease.[41]

Two of the earliest collections of instructions on penance are ascribed to Finnian and Gildas, both of them friends of Cadog. It thus seems possible that Cadog's foundation at Llancarfan influenced the development of spiritual direction in Ireland as well as the growth of monastic schools there. Gildas' letters reveal the historian of Britain's downfall as a gentler 'soul-friend' than his other writings might lead us to suspect. He is very critical of the 'arrogant contrivances' of those who indulge in too strict ascetic practices and remarks that 'Abstinence from bodily food is useless without charity.' He also recommends excommunication 'only in well proved cases of major sins.'[42]

It is tempting to draw parallels between the ideas of spiritual guidance in the Celtic Church and those which later developed among the eighteenth-century Welsh Methodists. William Williams' manual *Drws y Society Profiad* ('The Door of the Experience Society'), containing advice for those taking part in meetings in which they discussed their religious experiences and shortcomings, might well be thought of as a Methodist penitential. Similarly Dr Alethius, one of the characters in Williams' long poem *Theomemphus,* has much in common with a Celtic 'soul-friend'. It would however be misleading to stretch the comparison too far: confession in the Methodist society was made to the community of believers, rather than to an individual spiritual guide.

The tradition of contemplative prayer which began with the Celtic saints may seem to have largely disappeared from Welsh religious life with the Reformation, though it is perhaps significant that the Benedictine scholar Father Augustine Baker (1575-1641), author of *Sancta Sophia* or *Holy Wisdom,* a classic guide to the life of prayer, was a Welshman from Abergavenny who converted to Roman Catholicism.[43] However, the two writers who have ensured that the idea of mystical or contemplative prayer has not entirely vanished from the Welsh religious consciousness both come from the radical nonconformist tradition.

Morgan Llwyd (1619-59) became the minister of a gathered congregation in Wrexham after the Civil War and had some sympathy for the early Quakers, as well as being heavily influenced by the writings of the German mystic Jacob Boehme. His masterpiece, *Llyfr y Tri Aderyn* ('The Book of the Three Birds'), appeared in 1653. At one point the Eagle (Oliver Cromwell) and the Dove (Morgan Llwyd himself) discuss the inner life:

> Dove. *There are many voices in a man's heart. The noise of the world and its news, and its troubles, and its pleasures and its terrors. Inside the heart's room there is also the noise of thoughts, and disorders, and the ebb and flow of flesh and blood. And so the poor soul (like the drunkards' lodging) is full of clamour inside, one desire agitating the other, or like a fair or a great market where noise and talking and shouting fill the streets of the town within. This is the reason why a man does not know half his own thoughts, and why he does not hear aright what his own heart is saying.*

> Eagle. *But how can a man's mind be stilled?*

> Dove. *By going into the secret room, and that room is God himself within.* [44]

Many of Llwyd's religious attitudes and practices differed profoundly from those of the Welsh saints of the sixth and seventh centuries, but their understanding of the inner life of prayer had much in common.

A similar note is struck by the second writer, the Quaker poet Waldo Williams (1904-71). In *'Mewn Dau Gae'* ('In Two Fields') he describes the *'y llonyddwch mawr'* ('the great stillness') which came from a momentary encounter with God's reality:

> *Pwy sydd, ynghanol y rhwysg a'r rhemp?*
> *Pwy sydd yn sefyll ac yn cynnwys?*
> *Tyst pob tyst, cof pob cof, hoedl pob hoedl,*
> *Tawel ostegwr helbul hunan.* [45]

('Who is it, amidst the pomp and the excess? Who is it standing and containing? Witness of each witness, memory of each memory, life of each life, the quiet calmer of the self's trouble.')

Pennar Davies has described Waldo as 'a sporadic mystic' (*'cyfrinydd ysbeidiol'*) who was satisfied with moments (*'eiliadau'*) of insight. He says that the poet

> ... treasured the moment which like a shooting-star makes us wonderfully conscious of the mystery and vastness and glory of the universe, the moment which suddenly reveals a presence and suddenly enchants the heart, the second which makes true acquaintance shine. [46]

Waldo's mysticism included an awareness that within God's timelessness the centuries between our own time and the age of the saints could somehow be dissolved. On the centenary of the destruction of St Brynach's Church at Cwmyreglwys in a storm, he wrote a hymn which ends with a glorious and symbolic blending of the prayers of the sixth century hermit and the twentieth century Welsh worshippers:

> *Frynach Wyddel, edrych arnom,*
> *Llifed ein gweddïau ynghyd,*
> *Fel y codo'r muriau cadarn*
> *Uwch tymhestloedd moroedd byd.* [47]

('Brynach the Irishman, look upon us, may our prayers flow together, that the strong walls may be built above the storms of the world's seas.')

NOTES

[1] David W. James, *St. David's and Dewisland: A Social History* (Cardiff, 1981), p.17.

[2] Davies, *Wales in the Early Middle Ages*, p.155; Wade-Evans, *Vitae*, p.129.

[3] Henken, *The Welsh Saints*, pp.110-14.

[4] James, *Rhigyfarch's Life*, p.43.

[5] *The Liber Landavensis*, p.342.

[6] *Hen Gerddi Crefyddol*, edited by Henry Lewis (Cardiff, 1931), p.49.

[7] Wade-Evans, *Vitae*, p.xi.

[8] Wade-Evans, *Vitae*, pp.145, 147.

[9] E.G. Bowen, *Saints, Seaways and Settlements in the Celtic Lands* (Cardiff, 1969), pp.70-2; *Dictionnaire des Saints bretons*, p.70.

[10] James, *Rhigyfarch's Life*, pp.37-8.

[11] Taylor, *Life of St. Samson*, pp.45-6.

[12] *The Sayings of the Desert Fathers: The Alphabetical Collection*, translated by Benedicta Ward (London, 1975), p.88.

[13] Taylor, *Life of St. Samson*, p.45, note 5.

[14] F.E. Warren, *The Liturgy and Ritual of the Celtic Church*, edited by Jane Stevenson (Woodbridge, 1987), p.140.

[15] Gomer M. Roberts, *Portread o Ddiwygiwr* (Caernarfon, 1969), pp.18-20; Geoffrey F. Nuttall, *Howel Harris 1714-1773: The Last Enthusiast* (Cardiff, 1965, p.7; Eifion Evans, *Howel Harris, Evangelist* (Cardiff, 1974), pp.5-6.

[16] John Owen, *Coffhad am y Parch. Daniel Rowlands, gynt o Langeitho, Ceredigion* (Chester, 1839), p.34.

[17] Morris Williams ('Nicander'), *Y Flwyddyn Eglwysig: Myfyrdodau Priodol i'r Suliau a'r Gwyliau drwy'r Flwyddyn* (Bala, 1843), pp.142-3; *Emynau'r Eglwys* (Cardiff, 1960), p.256.

[18] Gwenallt, *Gwreiddiau*, pp.12-13.

[19] *Trioedd Ynys Prydein*, p.204.

[20] *The Liber Landavensis*, p.342.

[21] Baring Gould and Fisher, *Lives*, IV, 45.

[22] Warren, *Liturgy and Ritual*, pp.125, 127.

[23] Wade-Evans, *Vitae*, p.133.

[24] Taylor, *Life of St. Samson,* pp.20, 43, 45.

[25] James, *Rhigyfarch's Life,* p.36; *Dictionary of Welsh Biography,* p.838; *The Psalter and Martyrology of Ricemarch,* edited by Hugh Jackson Lawlor (London, 1914); Mark Redknap, *The Christian Celts: Treasures of Late Celtic Wales* (Cardiff, 1991), p.81.

[26] James, *Rhigyfarch's Life,* p.48; Warren, *Liturgy and Ritual,* p.lxxxiii; Silas M. Harris, *Saint David in the Liturgy* (Cardiff, 1940), p.12; Owain Tudor Edwards, *Matins, Lauds and Vespers for St David's Day* (Woodbridge, 1990), pp.163-7.

[27] Glanmor Williams, *The Welsh Church from Conquest to Reformation* (Cardiff, 1976), p.450.

[28] Williams, *Traddodiad Llenyddol Iwerddon,* pp.66-8.

[29] Meirion Pennar, *The Black Book of Carmarthen* (Felinfach, 1989), pp.11-12.

[30] *Llyfr Du Caerfyrddin,* p.16. A.O.H. Jarman points out (p.92) that '*A. kagell*' is an abbreviation of '*Ath uendicco de kagell.*' He notes that the same shortened form occurs in most of the following lines, and that the final '*a. h. G.*' is short for '*argluit hanpich Guell.*'

[31] V.E. Nash-Williams, *The Early Christian Monuments of Wales* (Cardiff, 1950), pp.66-7.

[32] Chitty, *The Desert a City,* p.4.

[33] Bowen, *Settlements,* p.140, *Dictionary of Welsh Biography,* p.908; Melville Richards, 'Places and Persons of the Early Welsh Church,' *The Welsh History Review/Cylchgrawn Hanes Cymru,* V (1970-1), p.340.

[34] Gerald of Wales, *The Journey through Wales,* p.190; Bowen, *Settlements,* pp.142-3.

[35] 'Carnarvonshire Antiquities,' *Archaeologia Cambrensis,* third series, VII (1861), p.147. See also Baring Gould and Fisher, *Lives,* IV, 178.

[36] Taylor, *Life of St. Samson,* p.42.

[37] Taylor, *Life of St. Samson,* p.37; Wade-Evans, *Vitae,* pp.63, 97.

[38] Wade-Evans, *Vitae,* p.97; Ryan, *Irish Monasticism,* p.109.

[39] John Morris Jones, *Caniadau* (Oxford, 1907), p.20.

[40] *Dictionary of Welsh Biography,* p.88.

[41] Kathleen Hughes, *Early Christian Ireland: Introduction to the Sources* (London, 1972), pp.84-5.

[42] Gildas, *The Ruin of Britain,* pp.80-2.

[43] *Dictionary of Welsh Biography,* pp.22-3.

[44] *Gweithiau Morgan Llwyd o Wynedd,* edited by Thomas E. Ellis (Bangor, 1899), p.232.

[45] Williams, *Dail Pren,* p.26.

[46] Pennar Davies, *Y Brenin Alltud* (Llandybie, 1974). It is almost impossible to convey the meaning of the final phrase of the quotation ('*yr eiliad sy'n gloywi'r adnabyddiaeth*') satisfactorily in English.

[47] *Beirdd Penfro,* edited by W. Rhys Nicholas (Llandysul, 1961), p.158.

CONCLUSION

I

The Cetlic Christian spirituality of Wales emerged out of the chaos and slaughter which followed the Roman withdrawal from Britain. It fused what remained of Romano-British Christianity with some of the deepest insights of pre-Christian Celtic religion and ideas and ideals drawn from the monasticism of the Christian East. Because of the essentially tribal nature of Welsh society, with its strong emphasis on the relationship between people and the place in which they live, this synthesis became earthed in the patterns of daily life (Dewi's 'little things'). The result was a spirituality which was domestic, communal, Incarnational and profoundly Christocentric, and yet which was also characterised by a capacity for moments of profound insight into the transfiguring glory of God in his creation.

The culture which provided the seed bed for this development remained (and remains) under threat. Augustine of Canterbury's arrogant contempt for the British/Welsh bishops is graphically described by Bede.[1] If the resulting ecclesiastical coercion was one problem, violent invaders continued to be another. Between them the Anglo-Saxons and the Vikings sacked the monastery and church at St David's twelve times in the period between 810 and 1089. Two of the bishops were among those killed in these raids.[2] The infighting which was characteristic of internal Welsh politics compounded these difficulties. Nevertheless the seeds sown in the 'Age of Saints' took root.

The reason for their survival is partly connected with the saints themselves. Enid Pierce Roberts has written that

> There was something very special about these people, a quietness and gentleness, something exceptionally loveable and lovely. Their names show that: observe how many of them begin with the prefix 'My-' or 'Ty-' or end with '-o' or '-io', prefixes and endings which convey affection. Bod-ty-wnnog (Botwnnog) was the foundation of our dear little Gwnnog, and Tygái was our dear little Cai; Tysul was a dear man born on a Sunday [*Sul*], and Tysilio would have been exceptionally likeable.[3]

The tribal groups among whom these saints settled came to regard them as very much their own. They saw themselves as the 'people' of the local saint. Their priest was also the saint's priest, his or her successor—sometimes linked by ties of blood because of the hereditary nature of priesthood in many rural areas. Thus the spirituality of the saints became integrated into daily living, and was able to persist quietly through the political and ecclesiastical upheavals of the centuries. Even now there are qualities and attitudes which survive in some Welsh-speaking rural communities which seem to have their origins in the tribal Christianity of the sixth and seventh centuries.

II

In *Hanes Ryw Gymro* ('The Story of some Welshman'), a play based on the life of the seventeenth century mystic Morgan Llwyd, John Gwilym Jones charts Llwyd's progress through the religious controversies of his age. By the end of the play Llwyd has reached a state of total disillusionment and despair. He pours out his agony in a desperate plea to God: '*O Dduw, tyrd, tyrd, tyrd â'th Angau gwyn i'm cusanu i a'm dwyn i i'th oleuni grisial Dy Hun!* ('O God, come, come, bring your holy Death to kiss me and take me to Your Own clear shining light!'). There is complete silence and then Llwyd's little son comes on to the stage. He calls to his father quietly and affectionately and Llwyd looks at him 'as though hearing a voice for the first time.' He stretches out his hand to the boy, who takes it. Then his small daughter comes in and calls to him, and he offers her his other hand. Morgan's wife then joins them, carrying her baby. She gives the child to her husband and, cradling the little one in his arms, he begins to sing her a nursery rhyme. The others join in. John Gwilym Jones tells us that the play should end on 'a note of quiet, affectionate joy.'[4]

The dramatist's message is that God will not be found in abstruse and bitter theological and political wrangling. He may, however, be found in the lovingkindness that is present in close human relationships at their best. When his son calls him, Llwyd recognizes the voice of love which is the voice of God. He sees that the things which he had thought significant, the agonizing soul-searching and the anguished spiritual quest with all its complex doctrinal confrontations, were really irrelevant. God was present not in them, but in the little family whom Llwyd had neglected and ignored for so long. The play provides a restatement of Dewi's emphasis on the 'little things,' pointing us towards the domestic, homely (*'cartrefol'*) aspect of Welsh spirituality, which in turn directs us to the Incarnation.

There has always been an Incarnational element in the Welsh tradition. It surfaced in the poetry of the thirteenth-century Franciscan Madog ap Gwallter, the *'Plygain'* carols sung early on Christmas morning in parts of Wales, and the hymns of Ann Griffiths which were partially influenced by those carols. More recently it has appeared in the work of poets like Alan Llwyd and Eirian Davies, one of whose *englynion* provides possibly its most perfect expression:

> *Ni wyddom am ddim rhyfeddach, —Crëwr*
> *Yn crïo mewn cadach,*
> *Yn Faban heb ei wannach,*
> *Duw yn y byd fel Dyn Bach.*[5]

('We know of nothing more wonderful: a Creator, crying, in a nappy. A Baby who could not be weaker: God in the world as a Little Child.')

This Incarnational understanding helps to break down the limitations of time and space, so that Christ can be present here and now in Wales, living out his life in our towns and villages as he once did in Palestine. Thus in Gwenallt's vision of *'Catholigrwydd'* ('Catholicity'):

> *. . . y mae Caerdydd cyn nesed â Chalfaria,*
> *A Bangor bob modfedd â Bethlehem,*
> *Gostegir y stormydd ym Mae Ceredigion,*
> *Ac ar bob stryd fe all y lloerigion*
> *Gael iechydwriaeth wrth odre Ei hem.*[6]

('. . . Cardiff is as near as Calvary, and Bangor every inch as Bethlehem, the storms ar stilled in Cardigan Bay, and on every street the lunatics can be healed and saved by the edge of his hem.')

III

he earthing of spirituality in the everyday is a characteristic of Celtic spirituality in general. Thus John Macquarrie writes of the religious traditions of the Scots Gaels:

The immanence of God in nature was certainly a strong feature, and no doubt it was easier to believe in that immanence when the world was not yet 'shop-soiled'. But perusal of typical Celtic poems and prayers makes it clear that God's presence was even more keenly felt in the daily round of human tasks and at the important junctures of human life. Getting up, kindling the fire, going to work, going to bed, as well as birth, marriage, settling in a new house, death, were occasions for recognizing the presence of God. All these things could be seen in two ways—as practical occasions to be dealt with, or, in a wider context, as signs of the all-encompassing mystery of God.[7]

The difference between the Welsh experience and that of the Gaels is a legacy of the traumatic period in which Britain became Wales. Both the Scots and the Irish Gaels have been through appalling experiences in more recent times: the Highland Clearances and the Irish Famine of the 1840s inflicted terrible suffering and desperately weakened Gaelic culture. For the Welsh, however, the sense of being embattled has its roots in the very time in which the Welsh language and culture came into being.

In religious terms the effect of this centuries old sense of being culturally besieged has been a degree of defensiveness and introversion that date back to the days when Bede berated the Christian British/ Welsh for making no attempt to convert their pagan English neighbours. The precious values of belonging to a place, a people, a religious tradition and a loving God, tied to a belief in the importance of mutual respect and lowliness rather than arrogance as the basis of human society, have often seemed (and been) threatened by an assertive, expansionist neighbouring culture. Paraxodically the result of this has been that many of the basic elements of the spirituality of the 'Age of the Saints' have been carefully preserved and cherished, albeit often without any conscious awareness of their origins, within the increasingly fragile and threatened society of Welsh-speaking rural Wales. This ancient spiritual legacy has a vital importance not just for Wales, but also for the wider world. It can still provide a pattern of hope for our present age just as it did in the chaos and confusion of the fifth and sixth centuries.

[1] Bede, *History,* pp.100-1.
[2] James, *St. David's and Dewisland,* p.19.
[3] Enid Pierce Roberts, *Dewi Sant* (Pwllheli, 1983), p.11.
[4] John Gwilym Jones, *Hanes Ryw Gymro* (Bangor, 1965), p.86.
[5] J. Eirian Davies, *Cân Galed* (Llandysul, 1974), p.18.
[6] Gwenallt, *Y Coed* (Llandysul, 1969), p.26.
[7] John Macquarrie, *Paths in Spirituality* (London, 1972), p.123.